D1116959

THE SIGNIFICANCE OF THE MESSAGE
OF THE RESURRECTION FOR FAITH IN
JESUS CHRIST

STUDIES IN BIBLICAL THEOLOGY

A series of monographs designed to provide clergy and laymen with the best work in biblical scholarship both in this country and abroad

STUDIES IN BIBLICAL THEOLOGY

Second Series · 8

THE SIGNIFICANCE OF THE MESSAGE OF THE RESURRECTION FOR FAITH IN JESUS CHRIST

Willi Marxsen   Ulrich Wilckens

Gerhard Delling   Hans-Georg Geyer

Edited, with an introduction, by
C. F. D. Moule

SCM PRESS LTD
BLOOMSBURY STREET LONDON

Essay 1 translated by Dorothea M. Barton.
The remainder translated by R. A. Wilson.

334 01500 6

First published in English in this edition 1968
by SCM Press Ltd
56 Bloomsbury Street London WC1
Second impression 1970

Printed in Great Britain by
Lewis Reprints Limited, Port Talbot, Glamorgan

CONTENTS

v

c. 2

ABBREVIATIONS

ET	*Expository Times*
EvTh	*Evangelische Theologie*
IDB	*The Interpreter's Dictionary of the Bible*
JNTS	*Journal of New Testament Studies*
LXX	Septuagint
RGG	*Die Religion in Geschichte und Gegenwart*
ST	*Studia Theologica*
TL	*Theologische Literaturzeitung*
TWNT	*Theologisches Wörterbuch zum Neuen Testament*
TZ	*Theologische Zeitschrift*
ZNW	*Zeitschrift für die neutestamentliche Wissenschaft*

INTRODUCTION

THE four essays here presented in translation speak for themselves. With the logical rigour and precision characteristic of German New Testament scholarship, the writers of the first three lead the reader through closely reasoned investigations of the scope and limits of the New Testament evidence for the Easter faith; and in the fourth, Professor Geyer offers a lucid analysis of various points of view on the matter among Continental scholars. If there were no more in this volume, it would be more than enough to set the reader thinking furiously and asking himself where he stands. But perhaps there is room, in an English edition of this valuable symposium, for a short essay reminding the reader of some of the more recent writing on the subject in the English language, and attempting some analysis of the problems as they present themselves to at least one observer on this side of the Channel.

This in no way purports to be an exhaustive review of the work of even recent English-speaking scholars on the resurrection. Rather, it is a free discussion of certain aspects of the subject with allusions to only one or two of the latest publications on it. But perhaps it is worth while to remember that a considerable library of twentieth-century books in English on the resurrection could be assembled;[1] and it would include, among many others, the widely different schools of thought represented by such names as the following (the order is alphabetical):

N. Clark, *Interpreting the Resurrection* (1967)
P. Gardner Smith, *The Narratives of the Resurrection: a Critical Study* (1926)
S. H. Hooke, *The Resurrection of Christ as History and Experience* (1967)
K. Lake, *The Historical Evidence for the Resurrection of Jesus Christ* (1907)

[1] *Theology*, LXX, No. 561 (March 1967) was also largely devoted to belief in the resurrection (sprung out of a conference at Birmingham in September 1966).

G. W. H. Lampe and D. M. MacKinnon, *The Resurrection: a dialogue between two Cambridge Professors in a secular age* (1966)
R. R. Niebuhr, *Resurrection and Historical Reason: a Study of Theological Method* (1957)
A. M. Ramsey, *The Resurrection of Christ: an Essay in Biblical Theology* (1945)
J. A. T. Robinson, 'The Resurrection in the NT', *IDB*, IV, pp. 43ff.
H. A. Williams, *Jesus and the Resurrection* (1951)

Now, among Christians who unite in affirming, as central to the Gospel, the final and absolute aliveness of Jesus after his death, the greatest cleavage in contemporary interpretations of this affirmation is between those, on the one side, who hold that the resurrection is the expression of a faith already reached by the first Christians, rather than its cause, and those, on the other side, who hold the opposite, namely, that the resurrection was the cause of a faith which did not previously exist: that is to say—to give it crude and inadequate and rough-and-ready expression—between so-called 'subjective' and 'objective' ideas of the resurrection. Of the former, Rudolf Bultmann is a conspicuous representative. He writes, for instance: 'If the event of Easter Day is in any sense an historical event additional to the event of the cross, it is nothing else than the rise of faith in the risen Lord, since it was this faith which led to the apostolic preaching.' (*Kerygma und Mythos* I, p. 47; ET, *Kerygma and Myth*, [1953], p. 42, see also p. 112 below.) For Bultmann, the Easter tradition, though based on a reality, is developed from a mistaken interpretation of that reality by the disciples. In England, which has been less influenced than the Continent by Rudolf Bultmann and all that he stands for, the 'objective' interpretation is, on the whole, the commoner. Neville Clark is speaking for many scholars in England (as well, indeed, as for some 'pre-' and 'post-Bultmannians' abroad) when he writes: '. . . the happenings to which the apostles bear witness are not finally to be explicated in terms of autosuggestion or strictly subjective experience. *They create faith; they are not its creation.*'[2] (Italics mine.) But even within the number of those who hold this (so-called 'objective') view, there is, again, a further division. This sub-division is between those, on the one hand,

---

[2] N. Clark, *Interpreting the Resurrection* (1967), p. 100.

who feel bound to leave without further definition the bridge
between Good Friday and Easter, and those, on the other hand,
who are concerned with some sort of name for this bridge. The
gulf, which is sometimes bridged, is defined—to quote him once
again—by N. Clark: 'In terms of historical investigation, the last
and indisputable facts which lie on either side of the Resurrection
are the death and burial of Jesus and the belief of the early Church
that he has risen. Between these two facts lies some reality which
seems to defy definition but demand explanation.[3]

G. W. H. Lampe, for one, is prepared (if I understand him
rightly) to let his faith rest wholly on the side of that gulf nearer
to us—the Easter side. By this I do not mean, of course, that he
does not include in the grounds of his faith the life and ministry
of Jesus, or that he does not insist emphatically that the Easter
Jesus is the *same* Jesus. I am referring here exclusively to the two
focal-points of the death, on the one side, and the aliveness on the
other. Professor Lampe rests his faith on the good evidence that
Jesus was found to be alive after his death. The claim made by a
large number of people that they saw Jesus alive cannot, he thinks,
have been due to mere hallucination, and must have been due to
something 'objective' having happened to those people. (He
rightly dislikes that question-begging word 'objective',[4] but it is a
convenient 'short-hand' symbol.) For this conclusion, he offers
two reasons: First, ... the context in which [the resurrection
appearances] seem, according to the records, to have taken place.
They seem to have come straight out of the blue and not in a
situation where anything of the kind might have been expected to
occur. Secondly, there is the consonance of that experience with
the subsequent experience of Christian people.[5] The experience
'changed all these people's lives and has gone on changing the
lives of people who try to understand it'.[6] The earliest and most
plausible evidence is enough, thinks Dr Lampe, to show 'that
there was an encounter, which they hadn't dreamed up for themselves, between the objective presence of Christ, "outside"
themselves, and their own selves'.[7] Thus, Dr Lampe expressly
dissociates himself[8] from the first major group already described

[3] *Ibid.*, p. 96.
[4] G. W. H. Lampe and D. M. MacKinnon, *The Resurrection: a dialogue
between two Cambridge Professors in a secular age* (1966), p. 20.
[5] *Ibid.*, pp. 19f.; cf. pp. 38f.
[6] *Ibid.*, p. 20.   [7] *Ibid.*, p. 21.   [8] *Ibid.*, p. 30.

—from those who hold that Jesus 'rose' only in the sense that his followers came to understand his true significance. No: 'There was an objective Easter event which produced the dramatic change in the outlook of the disciples.'[9] Again: 'The "Pentecostal" enthusiasm of the disciples arose, not from reflection about the value of a dead man's deed and words, but from the conviction that that man was alive as Lord and Messiah and that they could testify from their experience of actual encounter with him that God had glorified him.'[10]

Before pursuing this point further, it may be well to digress briefly to mention two of the more obvious problems arising from the resurrection narratives. It is usual now to abandon all harmonizing attempts to fit the resurrection stories of the four Gospels (not to mention the non-canonical Gospels) into a single, coherent narrative. It is usually assumed, in particular, that—not to mention irreconcilable details as between each of the stories—there is no reconciling even the whole block of Galilean with the block of Jerusalem appearances. The Galilean appearances belong to Mark (by implication at least—see 16.7), Matthew (except for an appearance to women, 28.9) and John 21; the Jerusalem appearances to Luke (and Acts), John 20, Matt. 28.9, and the appendix to Mark (16.9ff., by implication). I Cor. 15.1ff. names no locality. All these may bear valid witness to the conviction that Jesus was seen alive by his friends; but the topographical discrepancies are generally taken to suggest that the alleged setting of the appearances was something very much at the mercy of developing tradition; or, if Galilee is deemed to be the authentic, original context of these experiences, then the Jerusalem narratives are attributed to a tendentious desire to locate Christian beginnings there.

Of course, if the appearances were entirely 'subjective', or so 'spiritualized' as to be experienced simultaneously by different persons in different places and in different ways, then the genesis of different traditions presents little difficulty. But supposing 'objectivity' is taken to imply that Jesus could only appear in one place at a time, is it, after all, so impossible for holders of an 'objective' view to conceive of appearances taking place first in Jerusalem and then in Galilee—and, possibly, then once again in Jerusalem? The Eleven were all, it seems, Galileans. Therefore,

[9] *Ibid.*   [10] *Ibid.*, p. 31.

they were in Judaea only as pilgrims for the Passover Festival, as
Jesus himself had been. Within a short time (say, a week) of the
end of the Festival, they would naturally return to their homes in
Galilee. Why should it be impossible—if they really saw Jesus at
all—that some of them, at least, should see him first in Jerusalem,
and then in Galilee? Again, if one concedes that the appearances
occurred in time at all, there is no intrinsic reason why they
should not have been extended over an appreciable length of
time. And, if so, why should not some of them have taken place
at Jerusalem again *after* the forty or fifty days separating Passover
from the next Pilgrim Feast, Pentecost, for which the disciples
might have gone up to Jerusalem once more? Such literalism may
seem absurd; but it seems to make sense of the Marcan 'he goes
before you to Galilee' (16.7)—it would mean, when you return
home you will find him already there—and of the injunction in
Luke-Acts not to leave Jerusalem after Pentecost (Luke 24.49,
Acts 1.4)—it would mean, this time, do not return to Galilee, as
you did after Passover.

But the second problem is this. Even if we allow that, for forty
days or so, the disciples really did see Jesus from time to time
and that then, when they were back in Jerusalem again, the
appearances definitively ceased, why does Paul speak, in I Cor.
15.8, of his much later encounter with Christ as though it was
among, and continuous with, those Easter appearances? Does
not Paul, as the earliest datable writer in the New Testament,
indicate by this that the Evangelists, who wrote later, are objecti-
fying, localizing, and limiting what was really in the nature of
vision, with all the elusiveness and ubiquity of vision? For what
it is worth, the following observation may be offered. The decisive
cessation of the appearances in one final appearance (described by
Luke 24.51 (if the reading is correct) and by Acts 1.9 in terms of
ascension) was clearly something needed by the friends of Jesus
who had known him so closely as an earthly friend and intimate
that for them the problem was how to be weaned of this audio-
visual, quasi-physical relationship. A decisive withdrawal by
absolute cessation was, perhaps, for them the needed message.
For an opponent like Paul, by contrast, who, if he ever saw Jesus
during his earthly life, at any rate never knew him intimately like
the disciples, the reverse is needed. For Paul, the need is to be convinced of the reality of the glorified Lord and to be shown that he

is identical with the earthly Jesus whom the Nazarenes are follow-ing. If so, is it, perhaps, understandable that, when he had learnt this lesson, he should rank his vision among the early disciples' visions, as a vision of Jesus of Nazareth raised from death?[11]

So much, by way of digression, about two of the critical problems of the resurrection narratives. We return to discuss Professor Lampe's views. As we have seen, he denies mere 'subjectivity'. But when it comes to the question what distin-guished these encounters from, let us say, the conviction that any very great person is still alive and with us after he has departed this life, Dr Lampe is reluctant to specify—except in terms of the special and enduring effects of these encounters and, perhaps, their intensity. This does not mean that he has the slightest hesitation in affirming that there *is* a distinction. In a personal letter he writes as follows:

However vivid the memory of great men may be, even to the extent that we may wish to speak of 'feeling their presence round us', we are surely aware that we cannot use such language literally, i.e. to mean that we are actually here and now in their company. The disciples, I believe, knew themselves to be encountered by an actual living presence, and this was the presence of the Lord who was none other than the Jesus whom they had known, or, in the case of Paul, know of.

What places Dr Lampe in the former of my two subdivisions is therefore simply his reluctance to name the bridge between Good Friday and Easter other than in terms of the identity of the contemporary Lord with Jesus. He does not believe that the story of the empty tomb is to be taken literally, partly because, as a historian, he thinks that it rests on inferior evidence, and partly because, as a theologian, he repels any inference that the character of Christ's resurrection is different from that which, as Christians believe, belongs to those who are in Christ (whose bodies un-doubtedly decay and are destroyed).[12]

The other side of this 'sub-division' within the ranks of those who hold that the resurrection caused the Christians' faith rather than being caused by it comprises those who, in one way or another, give more weight to the affirmation that the tomb was empty. (This is what I call, namely, 'the bridge'.) Of these some

[11] See C. F. D. Moule 'Expository Problems: The Ascension—Acts 1.9', *ET* 68 (1956-57), pp. 205-9.
[12] Lampe and MacKinnon, *op. cit.*, pp. 58ff.

treat it, not literally, but as an indispensable symbol of something essential to the Easter faith, while others at least give serious consideration to it in its literal meaning also. N. Clark writes: '. . . the Empty Tomb stands as the massive sign that the eschatological deed of God is not outside this world of time and space or in despair of it, but has laid hold on it, penetrated deep into it, shattered it, and begun its transformation.'[13] And again: 'The narratives portray a continuity and a discontinuity. The continuity resides in the identity of the crucified Jesus with the risen Christ. Of this the Empty Tomb is the sign. The Resurrection is in body.'[14] W. Künneth (to go over to the Continent for a moment, though his position is far from typical there) appears to be saying the same when he writes:

. . . the empty tomb as a spatio-temporal datum is a symptom of the power exercised in the immanent world by the reality of the resurrection . . . The empty tomb . . . becomes the strongest expression of the Easter message's concern with the concrete, bodily resurrection, and at the same time the clear safeguard against every spiritualizing tendency to evaporate the central declarations of the resurrection. To that extent it is by no means a matter of indifference whether theology takes the empty tomb seriously . . .[15]

Both these scholars evidently see in the statement that the tomb was empty, even if it cannot now be taken literally, at least a way of affirming that the resurrection of Jesus was not independent of or detached from time-space events. Whether one can make that affirmation without also committing oneself to literalism is a matter to which we must return. But first, it is to be noted that, hand in hand with this opinion, goes the opinion (contrary to that of scholars like G. W. H. Lampe) that, whether or not we today can believe it in its literal sense, the tradition of the empty tomb is at any rate not a late accretion but is part of the earliest traditions. This view is clearly expressed by J. A. T. Robinson.[16] And W. Künneth, to take another example, is among those who believe that knowledge of the empty tomb is implied in the ἐτάφη of I Cor. 15.4. He quotes K. Bornhäuser with approval (in *Die Gebeine der Toten*, Gütersloh, 1921), as saying: 'It should

[13] Clark, *op. cit.*, p. 98.   [14] *Ibid.*, pp. 99f.
[15] W. Künneth, *The Theology of the Resurrection* (ET, 1965), p. 97.
[16] Robinson, *op. cit.*, pp. 45bf.

never have come to the point that in spite of the "he was buried" ... the phrase "he was raised again the third day" was understood in any other way than as raising from the tomb.'[17]

Before returning, therefore, to the theological questions, it may be profitable to pursue this question of the prevenance of the story of the empty tomb. Dr Lampe ably presents the case—it is a familiar case enough—for its having arisen at a comparatively late stage, as a way, simply, of affirming, against docetism, the real death and real aliveness of one and the same Jesus. The notion that the body actually emerged from the tomb was the only way at that time available of stressing the continuity and the identity between the Jesus who was crucified and the Jesus who lived; and the use of Ps. 16.10 ('thou wilt not suffer thy Holy One to see corruption') as a *testimonium* added momentum to the idea that the body of Jesus did not 'see corruption'.

But is it quite so simple? Here are some of the considerations that might give one pause. (1) Paul's ἐτάφη is, as has just been observed, felt by some to point decisively to Paul's knowledge of the story of the empty tomb. (2) The story is often accounted for simply by saying that a Jew of those times would not have been able to conceive of life after death except in terms of absolute continuity between the body laid in the tomb and the person who was known to be alive afterwards, and would therefore have been compelled to *assume* the emptiness of the tomb.[18] This may be; but it is worthwhile noticing that the story in its essentials is very far indeed from conforming to the presuppositions of Jewish apocalyptic. Jewish apocalyptic did not believe in a *permanent* raising from death until the End, which was still in the future. Before that, all that Pharisaic Jews could believe in, if they followed their normal premisses, was either that a man had been *temporarily* restored to *this* life (as in the raisings in the Elijah and Elisha sagas, or in the Christian stories of Jairus' daughter and Lazarus and others),[19] in which case, it was natural to assume that

---

[17] Künneth, *op. cit.*, p. 94, n. 52.

[18] W. Künneth, *loc. cit.*, is emphatic about this. As we have seen, he believes that the story was built into the earliest traditions; and, on the assumption of the Jewish manner of thought just described, this, indeed, is the only logical conclusion.

[19] And even in Matt. 27.52f., though practically all critics would agree in ranking this as a late and distinctively Christian legend. Note, also, Herod's idea that John the Baptist had risen, Mark 6.16.

it was the same body, or else that he had been seen in an immaterial spectre-like form—a belief well attested among Jews, from the story of the witch of Endor through the Book of Job to the Gospel allusion to the disciples' fright on the lake.[20] The story of the empty tomb, coupled with the clear evidence constituted by the various ways in which the Gospels (and the Acts) bring their tale to a close, shows that what was believed about Jesus was neither of these alternatives. Instead, it was that *the* final resurrection of the Last Day had somehow been anticipated in the case of Jesus alone; and, since this was a preposterously novel idea— indeed, clearly unthinkable, for any Jew who had not been compelled to it by experience—it is hardly logical to assume that the whole story is a tissue of materials moulded on a standard pattern. (3) If, however, for the sake of argument, we concede that a Jew must have assumed the tomb to be empty as soon as he was convinced that the dead man was alive, then the old-fashioned argument which asks, why, then, was the tomb not investigated by friend or foe and the body produced? becomes valid again. This is an argument which it is fashionable to dismiss scornfully.[21] But if, for a Jew, the aliveness of Jesus did stand or fall with the emptiness of the tomb, it is difficult to see what is wrong with the question. (4) Further, it is difficult to explain how a story that grew up late and took shape merely in accord with the supposed demands of apologetic came to be framed in terms almost exclusively of women witnesses, who, as such, were notoriously invalid witnesses according to Jewish principles of evidence. The later and the more fictitious the story, the harder it is to explain why the apostles are not brought to the forefront as witnesses.

Thus, the story of the empty tomb is not altogether easy to dismiss as a late, apologetic development. Neither, as has already been observed, is it easy to see how it can be a symbol of the involvement of the resurrection within time and space unless there is also something literally spatio-temporal about it. Perhaps, therefore, it is permissible to speculate, very tentatively, along the following lines. Literal belief in the empty tomb would mean that the material of which the body was composed was

[20] I Sam. 28; Job 4.16; Mark 6.49.
[21] Though see D. M. MacKinnon's view in Lampe and MacKinnon, *op. cit.*, p. 84.

somehow *transformed* into a different mode of existence (such as practically all Christians believe characterized the Jesus of the Easter experience).[22] It would mean that it was actually taken up into and superseded by the new mode, rather as fuel is used up into energy—though, in the case of fuel, it is admittedly not without remainder. Now, one thing is evident, namely, that this is *not* what happens to Christians or to any other human beings at present. Their bodies decompose; they are not transformed. Neither can a Christian of the present day entertain the bizarre idea (so popular in past ages) that the dissipated components of Christians long dead are, at the Last Day, to be reassembled so that they may be raised with the same bodies. No: But is it conceivable that the total matter of this time-space existence is destined by the Creator not to be 'scrapped' but to be used up into some other existence? This, it might be said, would imply a doctrine of creation, not *ex nihilo in nihil* (out of nothing into nothing), but *ex nihilo in aliquid novi* (out of nothing into something new); and the latter is certainly congruous with the idea of a God who never creates without a purpose. If so, is it inconceivable that in just the area of the body of Jesus, which alone had been surrendered to death in total absolute obedience to the will of God, this transformation and using up was anticipated; while with the rest of mankind their 'material' returns to the collective reservoir of the totality of matter one way or another, by decomposition slow or sudden, until this totality of things is ultimately used as the material of a new existence, in which they, by the grace of God, will share? If this were true, then the difference between Christ and believers (which Dr Lampe is anxious to avoid) would be only that Jesus *anticipates* their ultimate destiny.[23]

Perhaps this seems ludicrous—so ludicrous that one hardly dare formulate it. And yet what is the alternative? Only, I believe, to capitulate either to leaving the empty tomb out of the theological consideration or to accepting it as a symbol of time-space

[22] Perhaps, we may be excused from offering, at this point, one more specimen of the usual critical assessment of the degrees of physicality in the resurrection stories of the Gospels. There is no doubt that there is a traceable progression in the accounts, in respect of 'materiality'. Even if we harmonize the Galilean appearances with the Jerusalem appearances as such, this does not mean that such details are reconcilable.

[23] See C. F. D. Moule, 'St Paul and Dualism: the Pauline Conception of the Resurrection', *JNTS* 12.2 (Jan. 1966).

involvement without, however, elucidating what that involvement implies.

At any rate, here are some of the issues as they frame themselves for one observer in England—issues with which each reader must try to come to terms for himself. But underneath it all is the impressive fact that, in whatever camp one finds oneself, at any rate all who accept the evidence for the aliveness of Jesus after his death are *ipso facto* in agreement that this is the same Jesus who died. There may be those who declare that you have no right to faith in this continuity without in some sense including the empty tomb in your beliefs: nevertheless, the faith is there.

PREFACE TO THE GERMAN EDITION

THE contributions to the understanding of the resurrection by Professor G. Delling (Halle), Professor Geyer (Wuppertal), and Professor Wilckens (Berlin) which are here published, are papers which were read in the setting of the Theological Commission of the Evangelical Union Church. Those who gave them were asked to comment upon the article by Professor Marxsen of Münster, 'The Resurrection of Jesus as a Historical and Theological Problem'. This they did, sometimes explicitly, and sometimes without any express reference. Consequently, with the kind permission of the publisher and the author, who is also a member of the Theological Commission of the Evangelical Union Church, we have reprinted this study, which originally appeared separately, and have placed it before the other papers. The systematic review by Professor Geyer forms a conclusion. It gives a comprehensive summary of the various theological views which have been adopted, and formulates the questions which must be clarified or decided upon.

It will be worthwhile to give a brief account of how this inquiry came about.

At a session on the 30 January 1964, the Council of the Evangelical Union Church discussed the evident difficulties regarding preaching within the Protestant Church. When the justification and limits of political preaching are discussed, there is a frequent failure to bear in mind the perplexity at the very heart of Protestant preaching, especially in the understanding of the death and resurrection of Jesus.

With particular regard to the understanding of the death of Jesus, uncertainty prevails among the clergy, and especially among the younger generation. Is this death of intrinsic and fundamental importance in the sense that the crucified Jesus vicariously bore the judgment of God upon the sin of man? Or is such an understanding merely an interpretation made in the concepts of the particular age, which may well be replaced? Or again, it may be asked whether the death of Jesus has merely an exemplary significance in the sense that the crucified Jesus is not the object of faith, but the example of faith, showing us how it can be maintained even to death. Here again the understanding of the death of Jesus as having a constitutive function would have been abandoned; any example is merely explanatory, but not constitutive in its function.

With this situation in mind, the Council of the Evangelical Union Church asked its Theological Commission to concern itself with these problems, and if possible, to produce something which would aid the understanding of the death of Jesus, and which would be applicable to preaching.

Since one can only understand the meaning of the death of Jesus if from the very first one also considers the question of the significance of the resurrection, at its second session the Theological Commission came to discuss the problems dealt with in this work. It was inevitable that the fundamental questions posed above with regard to the understanding of the death of Jesus should also arise in discussing the problem of the meaning of the resurrection.

The papers which were read on the subject of the understanding of the resurrection are now being published. Further publications, dealing with the whole theme, 'The Understanding of the Death and Resurrection of Jesus' are to follow.

Fritz Viering

I

Willi Marxsen

THE RESURRECTION OF JESUS AS A HISTORICAL AND THEOLOGICAL PROBLEM

WHENEVER Christian theology concerns itself with the theme of the resurrection of Jesus, it raises at the same time the question of the foundations upon which the Church ultimately rests—and indeed the question of that foundation both in historical terms as well as in present fact. Paul has given almost classical expression to this in his argument with those Corinthians who denied the resurrection: 'If Christ has not been raised, then our preaching is in vain and your faith is in vain' (I Cor. 15.14). This means surely that apart from the resurrection of Jesus there would be no Church.

So it is quite understandable that the theme of the resurrection of Jesus has frequently been the subject of theological and historical scrutiny, and it has also frequently been the subject of theological and historical debate. This situation continues up to the present time. Indeed, we might actually say that the discussion is specifically concerned with the relation of the historical to the theological and of the theological to the historical.

Here we must note the fact that the problem (at least for *us* in the present day) is on a plane fundamentally different from that of New Testament times. For our relation to history since the Enlightenment has, after all, been different from that of the New Testament writers. It is important for us to pay much more attention to this than has frequently been the case, otherwise the discussion could easily fall into a Babylonian confusion of language resulting in the rising of uncertainties and misunderstandings which could have been avoided if the wording and the arguments had been expressed more precisely in the first place.

Let us illustrate this problem by an example from another sphere. The Evangelist John in writing his Gospel employed an earlier source of signs containing a series of miracles, some of

15

which were much more extreme than the miracles found in the Synoptists. If the Evangelist had been asked whether Jesus had actually performed these miracles, he would have assented to this question as a matter of course. A corresponding situation holds good in all respects for a large number of other occurrences which historical critical research must simply call unhistorical (if it wishes to remain honest). Now this implies methodologically that when we pass historical judgments we cannot subject ourselves to the belief held by the men of that time that these stories actually happened. We simply must (in spite of the unequivocal belief of those narrators and early readers) raise the question of historicity and then answer this question in accordance with *our own* historical judgment and knowledge. It is just this fact which seems to me important for us to realize, otherwise the debate would already be off to a false start.

Basically we have long been familiar with this method of reasoning even though it has been carried out in quite different field. Hardly anyone in the present day still holds the opinion that the world was created in six days. If we want to learn anything about how the world came into being, we turn to natural science, for it alone can give us information about this question. The conclusions of natural scientists do not indeed all agree, and are therefore 'disputable'. Nevertheless it will not occur to anyone to wish to overcome this uncertainty by means of the biblical story(ies) of the creation, nor, *vice versa*, can these refute the conclusions of natural science. Hence these conclusions can be reached only by means of research by natural science. Anyone who introduces methods inappropriate to the subject-matter under investigation ruins everything. It is true that natural science will undoubtedly never be able to affirm that the world came into being by creation, yet I can still speak of the creation in theological terms, even without depending on definite conclusions drawn from natural science.

Now we must be careful not to forget that this insight, familiar to us, required a very long time to make its way in the Church (against great resistance). Today hardly anyone calls it in question. And yet it seems to me important to draw attention to one more crucial point which is often unfortunately not sufficiently heeded.

It is customary to say that the account of the creation does not intend to assert *how* the world came into being, but *who* created the world. That is only partly correct. For, of course, the authors of the account of the creation were convinced that they were giving information that was also 'scientifically' accurate. When we say on the contrary that here we are *only* concerned with the fact that God created the world, we are thereby saying something which contradicts their 'scientific' belief. Thus out of a complicated 'scientific' and theological presentation we regard only the theological aspect as being correct, while at the same time we are no longer able to share the 'scientific' belief of the author, because natural science has its own methodology.

The present day discussion does not centre on the relation of the concerns of natural science to those of theology, but on the concerns of history to those of theology. We must now simply acknowledge that the scientific study of history, too, has its own methodology. Hence it must hold good analogously that in certain cases we may select out of a complicated 'historical' and theological presentation only the theological aspect as being accurate—even if we can no longer share the historical belief of those who held it. Thus if at times in the belief of the writers of the texts two aspects coincided, we cannot in the present day accept them both together without investigation. Yet at the same time we must realize that the theological aspect of the complicated statement under investigation need not be wrong, even if we can no longer admit its 'scientific' or 'historical' aspect.

Let us now apply this thesis to our problem. I think we shall quite quickly reach agreement if we pose the question as follows: What was the *belief* of the early witnesses (Paul and the early Church) with regard to what occurred at Jesus' resurrection? They obviously believed that it had actually occurred. Paul believed that here was an occurrence brought about by God. This follows quite unequivocally from the passage I Cor. 15.14 already mentioned. We can refer also to many other passages. One further example may be given. Paul in Corinth takes up the thesis ἀνάστασις νεκρῶν οὐκ ἔστιν (there is no resurrection of the dead) and reasons as follows: If (as a matter of principle) there is no resurrection of the dead, then naturally neither is there the special case, namely ,'the resurrection of Jesus' (I Cor. 15.12f.). Now undoubtedly Paul thought of the resurrection of the dead as a (future) *event* (cf. e.g. I Cor. 15.20ff.; 35ff.) and so the same must hold good also for the resurrection of Jesus (which had already occurred). And this belief of Paul was unquestionably shared by the early Church.

For the time being we will leave the matter at this point and turn for a moment to the current discussion. Now if we compare this general belief of the early Church with statements found in present day debate we cannot help noting important differences. Obviously this early Christian belief is no longer shared so unreservedly. From among several examples which might be cited I will adduce a quotation from Rudolf Bultmann out of his well-known university lecture at Heidelberg, at the end of which he wrote:

It is often said, most of the time in a criticism, that according to my interpretation of the kerygma Jesus had risen in the kerygma. I accept this proposition. It is entirely correct, assuming that it is properly understood. It presupposes that the kerygma itself is an eschatological event, and it expresses the fact that Jesus is really present in the kerygma, that it is *his* word which involves the hearer in the kerygma. If that is the case, then all speculations concerning the modes of being of the risen Jesus, all the narratives of the empty tomb and all the Easter legends, whatever elements of historical facts they may contain, and as true as they may be in their symbolic form, are of no consequence. To believe in the Christ present in the kerygma is the meaning of the Easter faith.[1]

It is evident that Bultmann deliberately pushes aside the question of what occurred at the resurrection (. . . whatever indication as to historical facts which they *may* contain), yet on the other hand he speaks of the Easter faith. Other similar statements (by Bultmann or others) could also be quoted, but this will suffice; for all that matters for the present is to propound the problem clearly.

The objection was raised against Bultmann in the ensuing debate that according to him the resurrection of Jesus was etherealized and then in practice abandoned. Opinions were expressed which were intended in the face of this to re-emphasize the fact, the occurrence, of Jesus' resurrection and to place it in the centre; on no account do they want to relinquish it. I think we must frankly admit that the desire shown here is intelligible.

[1] R. Bultmann, Das Verhältnis der urchristlichen Christusbotschaft zum historischen Jesus (1960), p. 27; ET, 'The Primitive Christian Kerygma and the Historical Jesus' in *The Historical Jesus and the Kerygmatic Christ*, eds. C. E. Braaten and Roy A. Harrisville (1964), p. 42.

For we simply cannot help asking whether, if we deliberately abandon the discussion about the occurrence of Jesus' resurrection, it is still at all possible to speak in adequate terms about what we are accustomed to call the Easter faith. Or in other words: Does it mean anything to say that Jesus is risen, if at the same time to declare the resurrection of Jesus as an actual event is unimportant?

On the other hand we must also realize that to abandon the attempt to take into account a particular (i.e. historical) aspect does not in the least signify that this aspect is altogether disputed as such. Bultmann is just not interested in it. But in that case the question may certainly be raised whether this lack of interest is really permitted if the discussion is not to be frustrated from the outset. And it is just this which is frequently brought up against Bultmann.

Without deciding whether this objection is justified or not, we will nevertheless investigate it and undertake the historical problem. Only we must be made aware that we are not allowed to make the matter as easy for ourselves as is only too often done.

It is, for instance, inadmissible merely to point out that the primitive Christian *kerygma* intends to convey a fact, and that therefore those who formulated this *kerygma* wished thereby (also) to affirm a fact. As we have said, there is no dispute on this point, however, in our context it is by no means a proof. For we are not allowed to take, by a short circuit, the belief of those who formulated the *kerygma* as a historical proof. It is impossible, in the sense of making a historical statement, for us to base our claim merely on the belief of those men (which must not be disputed, because it cannot be disputed) that the resurrection of Jesus did take place. On the contrary, we must investigate how Paul and how the Christian *kerygma* arrived at this belief.

Of course, it remains conceivable (and we must reckon with this possibility from the outset) that this can no longer be proved in historical terms. In that case we would certainly have even less right now to claim Jesus' resurrection directly (in the sense of establishing it as a fact in historical terms) as an event which had happened. In this case particularly we must take special pains to preserve the parenthesis—that we are concerned with a belief of Paul and the primitive community—and can really only speak of Jesus' resurrection in terms of its meaning in the *kerygma* and not in history. But it would be quite impermissible in view of such historical uncertainty to introduce the concept of faith since historical investigation into the facticity of an event cannot take refuge in faith.

Now it is of course obvious that I have *no* direct access to any event in the past. I have this access only indirectly through witnesses as intermediaries. Thus, strictly speaking, I must always make the reservation which I have just mentioned. If a witness gives me an account of a fact, then the facticity of this fact for me is always asserted by witnesses, never conveyed to me directly. And yet we must point out a real material difference here.

When Paul, for instance, in Gal. 2.11ff. speaks of his meeting with Peter in Antioch, he is talking about an event. Yet no one would wish to turn this passage into a problem like the one just mentioned. On the contrary, we accept it from Paul quite directly that this meeting was something which we, too, are ready to call an event. (It is true that we can interpret this event differently, and whether we adopt Paul's interpretation of it would be a separate question. But it is on another page, at any rate as we pursue our train of thought.) The nature of the event narrated in Gal. 2.11ff. as something which can be established in historical terms is *not* called in question, and no doubt *cannot* be called in question.

It might now be asked whether we are not inconsistent. In one case we accept Paul's belief unreservedly that he is speaking of an actual event; in another case we are not ready to do so (at least not so quickly). Where then does the difference lie between the event of the meeting in Antioch and the event (insofar as it was one) which Paul designates as Jesus' resurrection?

The difference does not lie in the fact, as we may perhaps sometimes hear or read, that we have to do in one case with something inherent in us, in another case with something divine; thus our question is now prompted by the *content* of what Paul understands as an event. Thus, for example, Walter Künneth says: 'As God's creative act which raised the crucified Jesus of Nazareth to a life of glory, this event stands beyond the inherent possibilities of human perception . . .'[2] Here a distinction is made between events within the range of human perception and others to which this does not apply.

[2] W. Künneth, in *RGG*, 3rd ed., I, col. 701.

At this point we must take quite special care that we are not led away by his methods from the straight path. Let us put the question as follows: If this event (i.e. the resurrection of Jesus) lies beyond the possibilities of inherent human perception, how then can we obtain knowledge of it? To this Künneth replies: 'Only the *spiritual* man possesses the possibility of perceiving the revelation awakened by God and the faculty of distinguishing between the divine and what is inherent in us.'[3] But now the matter becomes difficult. We can concede to Künneth that the spiritual man (as he calls him) sees more than the non-spiritual one, but how can this 'more' be defined more precisely? To begin with, both are, after all, facing the same historical phenomenon. I can of course say that the historical phenomenon, Jesus of Nazareth, has a twofold aspect or is ambiguous. Not flesh and blood, but only the Father in heaven could reveal that the encounter with this Jesus was an encounter with the Christ (cf. Matt. 16.17). Furthermore I can (perhaps in view of our gospels) establish the fact that witnesses who encountered this Jesus of Nazareth claim that they had come to know him as the Christ, and now express this knowledge. In doing so they are expressing something real which can only become something real for me too 'through the Father in heaven' (and that means spiritually). Without the Spirit I can only say: Men have claimed that they have come to know this reality; and without the Spirit contemporaries other than the disciples could only say: We saw merely Jesus.

But by means of spiritual perception no *event* is grasped, no historical fact, but merely the significance of a phenomenon open to others as well. Of this significance reality is a necessary characteristic. But this reality is recognized not *in addition to*, but precisely *in* the event.

Hence it must certainly be conceded that anyone who investigates in historical terms always reaches a more limited perception than one who claims to perceive spiritually. It remains hidden from historical perception that in Jesus' lifetime an encounter with him involved an encounter with God. Historical perception (i.e. historical exegesis) can always only state that witnesses claimed to have encountered God in Jesus. Whether this claim

[3] W. Künneth, *Glauben an Jesus? Die Begegnung der Christologie mit der modernen Existenz* (1962), p. 161.

proves to be true, exegesis is unable to determine. This was then and is today open only to spiritual perception, and in this sense we can call spiritual perception a more comprehensive perception. Only we must not express a spiritual perception in historical categories. But 'event' *is* a historical category. To speak of an 'event' beyond the inherent human possibilities of perception is to speak loosely because categories are being shifted.

But if the question is raised how the facticity of Jesus' resurrection is established, this can only be answered in historical terms. The historical verdict cannot be refuted in spiritual terms. And yet we must concede that the event may be more complex than historical investigation is able to perceive. But if the historical verdict is inadequate to express the complex whole, which we are contemplating, as comprehensively as it perhaps reveals itself to spiritual perception, then the historical verdict is not for that reason wrong if it is allowed to remain a historical one (and *merely* a historical one). We will leave the matter as such and continue our inquiry in historical terms.

I will recapitulate. We juxtaposed the *event*, that Paul met Peter in Antioch, and Paul's *belief* that Jesus' resurrection actually occurred. I asked: Why do we accept directly from Paul the event of his meeting with Peter, but see a problem in the other case. The answer *cannot* be (if we are asking about the event) that the content is different in each case (in the one it is about what is inherent in man, in the other about what is divine); rather it must be that Paul has in each case a different relation to what he considers to be an event. His meeting with Peter in Antioch happened to *himself* as an event. Therefore we accept from him directly the fact that this meeting took place and we ourselves are even ready to speak of it as an event. But the resurrection of Jesus did *not* happen to Paul directly as an event. Thus Paul himself has already a different relationship in each case to these two entities which he considers to be events.

We must not let our view of these existing differences be obscured by saying (according to current usage): But after all Paul did see the *Risen One*. *That* is what happened to him and therefore his belief that the resurrection had occurred is *also* based on what happened to him.

This is true insofar as Paul's belief that the resurrection took place is based on what happened to him. But this happening is not identical with the resurrection itself, as an occurrence of which he was a witness; what happened to him was that he saw someone. Now it is important to pay close attention to the one *whom* Paul saw. The apostle does not in fact say, as we easily formulate it, that he saw the *Risen One*, or that the *Risen One* had appeared to him. It is striking and worth noting that he uses a different expression. Let us look at the words employed.

When Paul speaks of what happened to him, what we call his experience on the Damascus road (and this is not at all identical with Jesus' resurrection), he says of it either that God revealed to him his *Son* (Paul does not say the Risen One [Gal. 1.15]); or he asks: 'Have I not seen *Jesus* our Lord?' (again he does not speak of the Risen One [I Cor. 9.1]). Only in I Cor. 15.8 is there a slight difference (but merely owing to the rest of the context). We read there: 'Last of all, as to one untimely born, he appeared also to me.' The position here is slightly different insofar as v. 8 is the last link in the chain of witnesses which is attached to vv. 3-5, thus to the *kerygma* which (also) deals with Jesus' resurrection. Now there is no doubt whatever that in vv. 3-7 (unlike v. 8) Paul was not just using his own words, but citing traditional material already handed on to him, which does not contain events which happened to the apostle. To *him* there happened merely an ὤφθη (he was seen, or else he let himself be seen, or else appeared, see below).

Thus it is worth noting that Paul when speaking of his Damascus experience speaks of a revealing, a seeing or an appearing of the Son of God, Jesus our Lord or else Christ—but *never* of the Risen One. Indeed, the resurrection terminology is not found at all in this context, which is directly concerned with what Paul had encountered. The reverse of this statement corresponds to it in a striking manner. When Paul speaks of the resurrection or the raising of Jesus (as he often does in his letters and in a variety of ways) he never does so as of something which had happened to him. Stated briefly: What had happened to him is never declared to be a resurrection; Paul never declares that the resurrection had happened to him. This consistency in the terminology seems very remarkable, especially as we pursue our problem. We shall have to investigate this matter more closely later.

But first we must ask how Paul came to understand as an event something which had never happened to himself. The answer may be completely unequivocal. Before Paul became a Christian and an apostle outside Damascus, he had heard the claim of the Christians: Jesus who was crucified is risen. What he then experienced outside Damascus brought him to believe that the claim of the Christians was correct. The belief that Jesus' resurrection had actually taken place is therefore founded for Paul *not* upon a happening of something which he considers to have taken place; on the contrary, it is a process of deduction. We are therefore on no account allowed to appeal to Paul if we want to describe Jesus' resurrection (directly) as an event which has happened, but we must begin by asking if this process of deduction is reliable. Hence we must not by a short circuit convert the belief of Paul into a historical judgment. If we wish to obtain a historical judgment (which we can use) we must inquire about the reason for the existence of this belief, and verify its existence.

But this can of course only be done by going back behind Paul and asking how the (pre-Pauline) primitive Christian *kerygma* arrived at the belief that Jesus' resurrection had in fact taken place.

Here a negative statement can at once be made which simplifies the problem materially: no individual of the primitive community ever claimed to have seen or experienced Jesus' resurrection as an event, a fact, a happening. This is found for the first time in the 'Gospel of Peter', in which the information is completely worthless as history.

Thus it follows that when the *kerygma* claims that the resurrection actually happened as an event (perhaps also by providing a date 'on the third day'), it is expressing a belief—or perhaps we ought to say more precisely that it is expressing *merely* a belief, without specifying witnesses, and what is more, without being in the least able to specify witnesses.

And so we must ask again (as in Paul's case) how this belief came into existence. Here we come up against two data: the empty tomb and the appearances of Jesus.

Let us begin with the tradition of *the empty tomb*. Attempts have been made to prove the historical truth of the empty tomb.[4] I certainly consider this attempt unsuccessful, but in our context this does not play a decisive role. For even if we are willing to

---

[4] Cf. for this in particular H. Freiherr von Campenhausen, *Der Ablauf der Osterereignisse und das leere Grab*, 2nd ed. (1958).

acknowledge as a possible statement in historical terms that Jesus' tomb was empty, nothing at all has in fact been thereby asserted about Jesus' resurrection. On the contrary, we should in that case have to do with a historical fact which not only *can* be interpreted differently, but also *has* been interpreted differently. It can be claimed that the disciples stole the corpse, that is why the tomb is empty (Matt. 27.64; 28.13; cf. John 20.13). But it can also be claimed that Jesus is risen, and that is why the grave is empty (Mark 16.6 and parallels).

When the question is put in historical terms, a limit is in any case reached. It is not possible to check the correctness of the (differing) interpretations. Now if I mention Jesus' resurrection in connexion with the empty tomb, then 'the resurrection of Jesus' is an interpretation and is intended to explain the existence of the fact that the tomb was empty. It is therefore not permissible (in connexion with a story about the empty tomb) to speak of the *event* of Jesus' resurrection, because it is not permissible to turn an interpretation into an objective fact; it is quite obvious that the empty tomb (even if its historical truth could be successfully proved) would be in no way a 'proof' of Jesus' resurrection.

At this point it is apparent that in the case of uncertain historical events we cannot take refuge in faith. Let us acknowledge that women stood before the empty tomb which is thus an object perceived by their physical senses. In order to ascertain this fact they need not resort to belief. The empty tomb was thus no 'object of faith'—and of course cannot become one later. To demand today, say, 'faith *in* the empty tomb' is a very inexact manner of speaking. In that case faith (today) is not directed towards the empty tomb itself, but 'trusts' the eye-witnesses for the reliability of their account in historical terms. Now this is something quite different. For in this case the question must be raised whether the earliest story of the empty tomb (Mark 16.1-6, 8) is in fact intended to be a historical account, or instead a particular form in which the resurrection was preached. I hold the second view. But even if that did not prove to be correct, this 'faith' in the reliability of the narrative in historical terms would always lead only to the fact of the empty tomb. But, as we have already mentioned, an interpretation in historical terms which cannot be checked but is merely stated, namely, that the tomb was empty because Jesus is risen, is ambiguous.

Closely analogous problems arise also with regard to the *appearances*. The traditions can be divided into two groups. In the first group only the *fact* of the appearances as such is mentioned; the second group is acquainted with *elaborate* tales of appearances (found particularly in the Gospels). In the latter Jesus speaks to his apostles, eats with them, passes through closed doors, etc. Now scholars have no doubt at all that the first group is older in terms of the history of the tradition than the second one. And further, there is agreement on the fact that the traditions handed on by Paul in I Cor. 15.5-7 belong to the earliest extant ones of this first group; they are probably to be regarded as the earliest altogether. The second group on the other hand represents a literary development of the first group. This means that at the beginning of the tradition there is the mere claim to have seen Jesus who was crucified.

The attempt has frequently been made at this point to take one further step forward by trying to discover something about the manner of this seeing. But in doing so two things must be kept apart much more strictly than what has often been the case. For first we can only ascertain how the seeing has been *described*. We would still need to examine as a second step whether we are able on the basis of this description to say anything about the seeing itself.

If we inquire how the seeing is described we must pay attention to the terminology. Although this is very varied, yet interest has frequently been centred on ὤφθη, a term which is undoubtedly pre-Pauline (thus very early) and one (among others) which is found also in formalized phrases of the traditional material (I Cor. 15.5, 6, 7, 8; Luke 24.34; cf. Acts 13.31, also Acts 9.17; 26.16). Here the translation already causes certain difficulties. ὤφθη (aorist passive of ὁρᾶν = to see) can be translated as (Christ) *was seen* (by Peter, etc.; the person being in each case in the dative). But in the passive form, ὤφθη, a deponent meaning is also possible.[5] In that case we might translate it as (Christ) *appeared* or *let himself be seen* or *showed himself*. Here there is a certain material difference insofar as in the first case the emphasis is, as it were, the activity of the witnesses, but in the other case the action is initiated

[5] F. Blass und A. Debrunner: *Grammatik des neutestamentlichen Griechisch*, 9th ed. (1954), §§191 (1); 313; ET, *A Greek Grammar of the New Testament and Other Early Christian Literature* (1961).

by Christ (*he* appeared). There is a third possibility, namely, to understand the passive as a form (common in Judaism) used as a paraphrase for the name of God. In that case we might translate 'God ... let himself be seen'.[6] It is hardly possible to establish the precise meaning with ultimate certainty from the form itself.

Nor do we get any further if we call upon other passages for comparison, because there are parallels for each of the possibilities mentioned. When Paul asks in I Cor. 9.1: 'Have I not seen Jesus our Lord', he is unequivocally speaking of *his* seeing. On the other hand the action of Christ can also be described instead. Thus, for example, we find in Acts 1.3: Jesus 'presented himself to them (the apostles) alive ... appearing to them'. W. Michaelis, who supports the second of the possible translations mentioned, expressed the opinion that here the subject alone is important, but that no particular weight is attached to the *seeing* by the witnesses.[7] To support this point he can certainly refer, e.g. to Gal. 1.16 where Paul is speaking of the fact that God *revealed* his Son to (Greek *in*) him, which undoubtedly indicates the Damascus experience. Only, in that case it is not in fact Christ, but God who is the subject. This would also provide us with evidence for the third possible translation. Moreover, I Cor. 9.1 makes it certain that the revelation of Gal. 1.16 was a seeing. That it was God who is here declared to be in action (quite apart from the passages mentioning the seeing) is made completely clear by the many statements in the New Testament which speak not of the resurrection, but of the raising of Jesus from the dead.

In this connection it seems to be important that with ὤφθη a phrase is brought into use which is often found in the Septuagint (the Greek translation of the Old Testament). This expresses the becoming visible, or the making visible by God of a reality which usually is hidden. Rengstorf has conjectured that the use of this phrase occurred for polemical and apologetic reasons. He supposes that the primitive community originally expressed the 'appearances' simply as a seeing without reflection in varied terminology. Then opponents tried to bring the happening into the sphere of a subjective experience of the disciples. The primitive community defended itself against this by taking up *deliber-*

---

[6] K. H. Rengstorf, *Die Auferstehung Jesu. Form. Art und Sinn der urchristlichen Osterbotschaft*, 4th ed. (1960), p. 57.

[7] W. Michaelis, *TWNT*, V, pp. 359, 6ff.

ately the concept of the Septuagint; and so here we meet 'the earliest protest of Christianity accessible to us, while it was still on the soil of the primitive community in Palestine, a protest against the attempt to divest the Easter event of its objective character and thereby to turn it from God's cause into that of the disciples'.[8] Whether this conjecture can be sustained seems to me doubtful. We should have to ask why this usage which had become necessary so early did not make its way more widely. Apologetics were certainly not less necessary later, but subsequent accounts of the seeing are given without this safeguard.

However, we can let this matter rest here. In any case we must say that, if we have a *deliberate* use of the term ὤφθη, the result has been to turn the interpretation of what happened at the seeing into a quite different direction. It can be an apologetic one; it can also be a theological interpretation (either with the help of the usage in the Septuagint, or more generally by paraphrasing the name of God by means of the passive mood).

The *description* of the seeing which is claimed to have happened is varied. We are merely able to recognize incidental interpretations of the seeing in definite directions. Yet it could not be gathered from what actually happened that it was a matter of a happening brought about by *God*. Hence such a statement is only an interpretative statement.

For this reason we must be extremely cautious if we want to describe the seeing itself more fully or even to explain it. Do the descriptions in fact suffice for what they are intended incidentally to produce?

A *hypothesis of a subjective vision* (such as frequently crops up in recent times since David Friedrich Strauss) is meant to transfer the visions into the disciples' hearts and minds; thus it understands them in the last resort as the result of their faith. Here the judgment of the historian must be that the possibility of such an explanation cannot be excluded. Yet it cannot in any way be proved. But if we accept it, we shall at once be thrown back onto the description by those who narrate the visions exactly as something that happened and thus clearly offer another explanation themselves. We simply do not get any further than the statement that the seeing has been *claimed* as something which took place.

[8] K. H. Rengstorf, *op. cit.*, p. 58.

If we go beyond this we are making a synthesis, yet without being able to appeal to any text.

This must also be emphasized against a so-called *hypothesis of an objective vision*, such as has recently been mooted, for example, by Hans Grass.[9] Grass does indeed call this hypothesis a 'theological and not a historical one' (p. 248), and thus we should not really need to examine it at all in this context (in which we are deliberately raising questions in historical terms). But what is unfortunate in Grass' train of thought is the fact that he does, after all, arrive by way of 'faith' at a statement about something like events. It is just for this reason that we must at least touch upon the problem here. Grass says: 'Theological considerations must hold fast to the fact that, as regards the experiences of the disciples by whatever means they are thought to have been communicated, we are concerned with God's action on them and not merely with the products of their own imagination or reflection' (p. 243). But must this really be admitted? Of course we cannot dispute the fact that the disciples could understand their experiences as God's action and declared them to be so. Even if they did not always say so *expressis verbis*, we can ascribe this to them throughout. However, can I also by 'theological considerations' come to speak of God's action? Surely not! Then what am *I* considering? Surely not the events themselves, but (interpreted) descriptions of what happened at the seeing. Grass is simply establishing a false relationship here by omitting the description and wishing to be guided directly by the events themselves. But since no one in the present day witnessed these visions, how can a believer in *the present day* 'see God's action in the visions of the disciples' (pp. 244f.)?

Grass admits that visionary experiences are ambiguous, and he is quite right in saying that faith alone prevails over ambiguity (p. 244). However, present day faith cannot overcome the ambiguity in visionary experiences *of those days*. Or does faith, after all, once again become a means of knowing about a *happening* which otherwise remains inaccessible? Grass seems to hold this opinion, else he could hardly have written: 'It is to God's action in relation to Christ *before* all his action in relation to the apostolic witnesses and *before* all his action in relation to us through the witness of his witnesses, action which thereafter is the foundation

[9] H. Grass, *Ostergeschehen und Osterberichte*, 2nd ed. (1962), pp. 233ff.

of the Church's preaching, that we must hold fast' (p. 246). Is not the process of seeing being examined here carried out in reference to its (possible) presupposition which is *supposed* to be ('considered theologically') God's action? But faith (our faith) must hold fast to this supposition, even though 'God's action with regard to Christ at Easter in the last resort withdraws itself from that possibility of being checked and stated objectively which might establish and verify the event(!) even apart from faith' (p. 246). Thus the *event* which preceded the (verifiable, in itself ambiguous) happening is accessible to faith.

We must ask again—how can *our* faith achieve this certainty with regard to the event? How can *we* believe that 'in the case of the visions there was no self-deception on the part of the disciples to be explained by presuppositions of their own, but that God acted here and did not leave Christ to die, but restored him to life . . .' (p. 249)? If we look at this more carefully, we discover where the mistake is to be found. In the case of the subjective-vision hypothesis it is the disciples who, so to speak, create the visions by their faith; on the other hand, in the case of the objective-vision hypothesis it is the faith *of today* which relies on objective visions. Thus the so-called objective-vision theory when examined closely is a subjective one *too*, i.e. it is derived from our own faith. But it is always a matter of synthesis which attempts to penetrate into a sphere lying beyond the range of the statements of the first witnesses. At the same time the interpretation given by the disciples to what happened to them is usually quietly turned into history. Therefore it is not advisable to proceed along this road.

Hence we may conclude as follows: We can say quite confidently that it did happen that witnesses saw Jesus who was crucified. We must express it more precisely. Witnesses claim, after the death of Jesus, to have seen *him*, and it is just this vision which they express in different ways, partly already with incipient interpretations of what they saw. On the basis of this vision, which witnesses claim to have happened to them, they then, by a process of reflective interpretation, arrived at the statement: Jesus has been raised by God, he is risen. *At that time* they naturally also took the view that they were speaking of an event which had really taken place. They were now convinced that the resurrection of Jesus had taken place.

But today we are *no longer* in a position to speak so directly of the resurrection of Jesus as an *event*; we *must* simply say: *We are concerned with an interpretative statement* made use of by those who reflected on what had happened to them (at that time!). Hence if today we raise the question in *historical* terms (!): Is Jesus risen?— we can only reply: That cannot be established. (*In historical terms it can only be established* (though quite reliably) that witnesses, after the death of Jesus, claimed that something had happened to them which they described as seeing Jesus, and reflection on this experience led them to the *interpretation* that Jesus had been raised from the dead.

Now I have already said that in certain circumstances a phenomenon will not reveal itself in its complexity when considered in purely historical terms. So we must ask whether this phenomenon which we have now worked out and which we can comprehend in historical terms, namely, a claim to a vision, is after all indeed the whole truth of what really happened. We must note carefully the fact that we cannot ask this question *directly*, for none of us are in a position to have direct access to this actual vision which the witnesses claimed. We cannot, therefore (in order to make use once again of earlier ideas) supplement our questioning about Jesus' resurrection in historical terms with questioning in so-called spiritual terms, in order to be able to regard (perhaps by spiritual means) his resurrection as an event. And it is just as difficult on the basis of *our* faith to penetrate now by means of theological considerations into what has been established in historical terms. How can we nevertheless proceed further?

I think that this is possible only if we continue our questioning once again in historical terms, but endeavour to enlarge the angle of approach. With regard to a past historical fact we can always learn only as much as has been handed on by tradition (and in our case this means by texts). Now we have already seen that not only the fact (that the vision happened) had been handed on as such, but that it was interpreted at the same time as an appearing of one raised from the dead. We endeavoured first to concentrate our interest on the event itself; we are now concerned to obtain a somewhat closer view of the relationship between this event on the one hand, and the interpretative statement employed on the other. Here again our faith cannot take us any further; we must question the texts.

I begin with a statement of Ulrich Wilckens.[10] He says that the witnesses who had had the experience of this happening were obliged to make it known 'with the resources of the tradition'. And the fact which Wilckens adds in 'parentheses' must be taken for granted, and deserves not only to be emphasized, but also to be pondered, namely, that these witnesses had no other means of expressing themselves than those which their tradition placed at their disposal (p. 89). But just on that account we must be a little more careful than Wilckens in applying this true insight.

In this matter we should not let ourselves be deceived by the quantity of what is reported, nor in particular by later developments. Without any doubt the situation is that the experience of the appearance was being pondered, at first mainly, later almost exclusively, with the help of the interpretative derivation, namely, 'resurrection'. But the very fact that this happens frequently at the beginning, and the effective victory of this interpretative derivation in the history of the tradition (then indeed detached from what had happened) should not induce us to regard this interpretative derivation as the *only possible* one, which is so closely connected with what happened that it *cannot* in any way be separated from it.

The fact that Wilckens (rightly) distinguishes between what happened and the resources of the tradition, with the help of which the happening was made known, hints at a possibility which Wilckens oddly enough does not discuss at all. For we ought to raise now the question whether the same happening could not under certain circumstances have been interpreted and made known with the help of quite different categories and images (which were also available)—could not in fact have been interpreted quite differently. In any case, in this connexion we must consider whether we are today absolutely tied to the interpretative derivation of that time. But I should like to put aside considerations about the principles of interpretation, and remain in the sphere of historical questioning, especially since at this point an answer to the question we have raised comes into view.

---

[10] U. Wilckens, 'Der Ursprung der Überlieferung der Erscheinungen des Auferstandenen', in *Dogma und Denkstrukturen*, ed. W. Joest und W. Pannenberg (1963), pp. 56ff.

We have already seen that Paul, when speaking of what happened to him, did not use the established resurrection terminology available to him (and only in I Cor. 15.8 was there a certain connexion with the resurrection insofar as it is mentioned in the *kerygma, before* the list of witnesses). But the list of witnesses itself is instructive. It has, as we know, several items, and the division between the pre-Pauline material and the Pauline supplement cannot be drawn quite reliably. But in any case we have here (whether earlier than Paul or by Paul himself) a supplementary revision of several traditional phrases which mention in each case an ὤφθη followed by the names of the witnesses of this ὤφθη, namely, Peter, the Twelve, then more than five-hundred brethren, then James and all the apostles, and lastly Paul.

In the context of I Cor. 15 no doubt Paul is probably concerned to refute the thesis of the opponents that there is no resurrection of the dead (v. 12) by referring to the uniform primitive Christian preaching: 'Whether then it was I or they, so we preach and so you believed' (v. 11). But what meaning was there originally in individual traditions worked in here, if it was asserted of definite people in the primitive community that they had seen Jesus after his crucifixion?

Peter was undoubtedly (at least at first) leader of the primitive community. If he is thus emphatically held up as the first to whom an appearance was granted (I Cor. 15.5; Luke 24.34), his activity as leader may have been based on this very fact. The statement that Jesus appeared to all the apostles provides the basis for the fact that only those who have seen Jesus after his crucifixion (cf. also I Cor. 9.1) can be apostles (according to that early usage). On the other hand, not everyone who has seen him is therefore an apostle. Thus the mention of the appearance to more than five-hundred brethren at one time may point to the foundation of the post-Easter community. The authorization-formula for James confirms his position as community leader, which had (later) passed to him from Peter (cf. Gal. 2.12). To sum up, we may therefore say: On the basis of the appearances there existed both the community (more than five-hundred brethren) and its oversight by Peter, the 'office' of the Twelve and the office (not to be identified with it!) of the apostles, as well as—later—the oversight by James.

Insofar as Wilckens points *to these facts* we must agree with him.

But it all becomes inaccurate when he expresses himself as follows: 'It was a matter (i.e. in the case of the individual traditions before they were edited) of hastily gathered formulae of a sacral legal nature with the object of mentioning the bare fact of Jesus' resurrection and appearance to those Christians who were thereby called and authorized to be leaders' (p. 81).

As we have said, this is inaccurate; for in the individual phrases of the tradition put together here it is not the fact of the resurrection which is mentioned, but *only* the appearances. It is *these*, rather than the resurrection, which are understood as authorization. Wilckens does indeed think that the individual formulae of authorization may 'have been briefly preceded by the announcement of the resurrection' (p. 75). This can be neither proved nor refuted. In any case, Wilckens can only appeal for this conjecture to the editorial sequence of I Cor. 15.3-7 as well as to Luke 24.34. Yet even then, what actually gives the authorization would still be the appearance; the mention (even though it is placed first) of the resurrection would be the additional explanation for the possibility of the appearance.

Here we merely get into trouble if (according to our current usage) we speak thoughtlessly of the appearances of the *Risen One* without bearing in mind that he who was seen, namely, Jesus, could be designated as the Risen One only as the result of reflection. Therefore we ought (and this applies as a matter of principle) always to consider very carefully when speaking of the appearances whether it is permissible to speak of the appearances of the *Risen One*, or whether we ought not to speak more correctly of the appearances of *Jesus*. On this point the context must each time be examined closely, and as a result we shall have to speak of the appearances of Jesus in each case.

Hence we affirm as follows: The formulae show that both the setting up of the community as well as the reasons given for functioning within it were traced back to a vision of Jesus after his crucifixion. Now this means that what supplies the real basis of the community and the functions within it is *the fact*, not of the resurrection itself, but of Jesus' *appearances*; this fact alone is brought into prominence.

But if the appearances of Jesus (as they were asserted) on the one hand led to setting up the community, and on the other also brought into being a function within it, then these are likewise interpretative derivations, for they were originally connected with the appearances and seemed to derive from them. This is seen quite clearly in Paul, most clearly perhaps in I Cor. 9.1. Here Paul is concerned to claim that his apostleship sprang from the same origin as that of the other apostles. That is why he asks: 'Am I not free? Am I not an apostle?' And then he substantiates this claim of his with the question: 'Have I not seen Jesus our Lord?' Thus the position is that, at least for Paul, his vision (and his vision *alone*) substantiates his apostleship.

It is true that in Gal. 1.15f. the experience of Damascus is not described as a vision but as a revelation. Yet here too exactly the same association can be recognized: 'But when he who had set me apart before I was born and had called me through his grace was pleased to reveal his Son to me *in order that* I might preach him among the Gentiles . . .' The position is again that what happened to him brings into being a function. It is not certain whether we may mention II Cor. 4.6 in this connexion although it might perhaps be fitted in here as being pertinent to the point.

But Paul is not alone in tracing his mission to his vision of Jesus. In the conclusion of Matthew (28.16ff.), which quite certainly conceals older traditions behind its present form, the appearance is involved in the sending expressed in the missionary charge. The resurrection terminology is missing here. Something similar can be observed in John 20.19-23. Jesus (who is again not designated as the Risen One) comes to the disciples, vouches for himself, so to speak, by showing his hands and his side (for the purpose of identification), breathes on the disciples and sends them out. Later in the context of the sending the other interpretative derivation, namely, 'resurrection', is indeed mentioned as well, but its origin has nevertheless persisted even though it was to some degree developed by reflection. This may be illustrated by Acts 10.40-42. In Peter's speech we read: 'God raised him (Jesus) on the third day and made him manifest; *not to all the people*, but to us who were chosen by God as witnesses, who ate and drank with him after he rose from the dead.' And *he commanded us to preach* to the people (and to testify) that he is the one ordained by God to be judge of the living and the dead. We have here, it is true, a Lucan revision of the tradition, yet the theme of sending has been preserved, and the reason is given for the restriction of the appearance to a small circle. We must indeed always bear in mind that the appearance was not a happening available to everyone. On the contrary, it befell (with the exception of Paul) only those, or more precisely it was only claimed by those, who knew the earthly Jesus. After all they alone were in a position to confirm the identity of the one whom they saw with the one whom they knew before.

We can therefore state that the experience of the appearances came to be spoken of in two ways. Although these interpretative derivations were later combined together, permeate each other mutually and form one sequence, namely, resurrection (appearance)—mission, yet it remains sufficiently clear that they once existed relatively independent side by side. They both belong from the outset to the complex understanding of the appearance which was experienced by them, or, in other words, the experience of the vision is found in two explanatory contexts, each of which points in a different direction. But in that case it is striking that it was not *necessary* for the experience of the vision to be combined, without qualification and each time, with what was interpreted as the resurrection of Jesus. It was therefore altogether possible to affirm the complex reality of what had happened in such a manner that Jesus' resurrection was not explicitly mentioned.

We will now compare the two interpretative derivations, and in doing so we will take note of two things: First, the *direction* of each interpretation; and second, the *content* of what is interpreted.

First, let us examine the *direction*. If what occurred when Jesus was seen is interpreted as 'he has been raised', then one might say we were going *back in time*. The question is: How could this occurrence of the vision of Jesus ever have come about? This itself is a matter of reflection. The conception of an expected raising of the dead at the end of time is well known. It was already in existence and was in fact still disputed in Judaism in Jesus' lifetime. It had prevailed against the opposition of the Sadducees, and probably Jesus himself accepted it (cf. Mark 12.18-27). Now if a man who has died is seen alive, it is quite natural to take up this conception and to assert that the expected raising (actually still awaited) had already occurred in the case of Jesus.

But in the second case the position is different. No real reflection takes place here. No inference is made back from what had happened. We are led in the opposite direction, the experience brings into being a *function*. If the question is raised (as, for instance, by Paul in I Cor. 9.1) about the evidence for this func-- tion (in Paul's case the question about the evidence for his apostleship), attention is drawn to his having seen Jesus after his crucifixion, but *no* reference is made to Jesus' resurrection.

Thus we can state that both the reflection and the function have a common starting point, namely, the claim that the appearances had occurred. But what had occurred 'came to be spoken of' in opposite directions.

We must now consider the question of the *contents* of what has been interpreted and will begin with the second interpretative derivation which we describe as bringing into being a function. The old traditional phrases (the pre-Pauline ones in I Cor. 15 and the Pauline ones) are very terse and thus present some difficulty. Besides, they are found only in the context which substantiates functions already actually being carried out. Just for this reason it is not an altogether simple matter to specify the content of what *constitutes* these functions. As regards their form, it was probably in the first place a question of preaching. Yet the content of this preaching is not the experience of the appearance of Jesus which brings into being a function. Nor did the vision itself provide the witnesses with a *fresh* content to preach, or *fresh* revelations which need to be handed on and which now made this vision and what was connected with it to be the central content of the preaching. The content is rather, as Jesus is reported to have said later in the Gospel of John: 'As the Father has sent *me*, even so I send *you*' (20.21).

Hence Jesus' 'purpose', having been set in motion by the vision which was experienced, was being carried on (if I may sum it up in these terms; we will examine this more closely later). It is carried on by his witnesses. In their function they now take the place of Jesus. They substantiate their right to further this purpose by claiming that they had seen Jesus after his crucifixion.

In this connexion I think we must simply agree with the proposition: 'Jesus rose into the *kerygma*', even though its terminology is incorrect. But Bultmann[11] himself says that this proposition must be understood rightly; so he interprets it at

[11] Bultmann, *op. cit.*, p. 27; ET, p. 42.

once, and in doing so he modifies it by not repeating the concept of 'rising again'. According to Bultmann the proposition must be understood to mean 'that Jesus is really present in the kerygma, and that it is *his* word which involves the hearer in the kerygma'; and in fact there is meaning in this proposition only in this sense; for if 'resurrection' is mentioned in the *kerygma*, then a theme of the other interpretative derivation is taken up, that theme which (at least at the beginning) did not occur at all in what had been our interpretation. For this very reason we shall not speak of 'resurrection into the kerygma', for then we are using the term resurrection in a manner so much modified that it no longer means what it was originally (especially in Jewish apocalyptic) intended to express. Hence it is not a question of bringing *resurrection* into the *kerygma*, but of Jesus' presence in the *kerygma* of his witnesses, of the *living* presence of the Jesus who was crucified.

Thus we can, in the first instance and provisionally, declare the content of the function brought into being by the vision to be that the purpose of Jesus is continued. What is at stake is that Jesus' *kerygma* continues to be preached. However, a new element appears, namely, that the continuation of the preaching occurs without the earthly Jesus being visible or present. And this takes place in such a manner that the old 'purpose' brought by Jesus is also not considered apart from him. The witnesses do not produce from it any idea, any truths which could be dissociated from him, no ideology and no religion; but the continuing occurrence of the Jesus' *kerygma* always remains the continuing occurrence of the *kerygma of Jesus*.

This becomes evident, for instance, in the synoptic tradition. The *logia* source, in particular (and also plenty of other detached material), contains no Easter stories nor allusions to what happened after Good Friday. Here, what I have just described as the continued furtherance of the 'purpose' of Jesus simply *happens* (in the preaching of the *kerygma* by the witnesses). The act which set in motion this continuance is not explained, still less is it reflected upon. By making a change in Bultmann's phraseology we might formulate it as follows: The fact (*the fact* that this tradition exists *as the kerygma*, more precisely: that this tradition exists *as the kerygma after Good Friday*) indeed implies that the vision was experienced.

We might sum up briefly by saying that the content of the

interpretative theory that the appearances bring into being a function, is that *he still comes today*. And because what matters is that *he*—comes *today*, even though we are guided by what *he* did in the past, at the same time we are free to modify the traditional material to suit the ever fresh present, as we can gather very clearly from the history of the synoptic tradition. For *he* indeed comes—*today*.

Now we must consider the other interpretative derivation. Here what happened is reflected upon, and thereby fresh contents do in fact come into being. I have already mentioned that an existing conception is taken up, namely, the (well-known) conception of the resurrection of the dead. Because the vision was experienced, the witnesses thus proclaimed that Jesus had been raised from the dead. But what does that mean?

The immediate answer can be that in this case a function is *not* (at least *not* directly) carried on to the end, but reflection is directed towards the one who brought into being a function towards Jesus. We have not a statement about functions but a statement about a *person*. To this extent we have here that stage in the development of christology which, starting with statements about functions, makes ever more statements about a person. Probably the starting point for this development really lies here.

Now we might end with this statement that reflection is directed towards the one who had previously brought into being functions. By this means at any rate two things would already be achieved. First, by interpretation based on reflection a *datum* is assumed: God raised Jesus to life after three days. Next, Jesus who was crucified is identified as Jesus who had been raised. Only we must be quite clear about the fact that both these are assumptions reached by reflections. What can be done with these assumptions, or more precisely, what could be done *later* with these assumptions?

Fundamentally, nothing at all; for these assumptions could at best supply information concerning the *belief* of those who had carried out (with the aid of *their* conceptions) this process of reflection. Now we must on no account confuse two things with each other. We are not receiving information here concerning *matters of fact*, but concerning a *belief*, and indeed a belief about which we can perceive two things. On the one hand we can see how it was brought about (by means of seeing Jesus who was

crucified), and on the other hand we can also completely understand its origin (because we know the existing conception which
was used). Thus if these assumptions can give us information
concerning the *belief-of those* who had carried out this process of
reflection, then this belief strikes and concerns others only when
the reflection once again brings into being a function. This could,
for example, occur if I followed up the belief of those people and
said: *Because* Jesus was raised from the dead by God and is therefore the Risen One, therefore he did not remain dead, therefore
he is alive, therefore his 'purpose' did not come to an end with his
death, therefore what he brought is not simply a thing of the past
and lost to the past, but *it still holds good today*. Thus if I say:
Jesus has been raised from the dead, then this belief (obtained by
means of thought) of the first witnesses is (now quite literally)
un-interesting unless I say *at the same time*: He is the Risen One
because he (identical with the earthly one) still *comes* today with
the same (old) claim. But if I say this then I must understand
clearly that I need no longer accept the concept of 'the Risen One'
unreservedly, but must speak of the 'Living One'. And that after
all is actually more; for he is only designated as the 'Risen One'
in a conception already in use in the history of religion; in doing
so we bring into relief from one side only the conception, already
in use in this connexion, of the entry of the crucified one into life.

Now what was achieved by reflection at that time cannot
merely represent a piece of neutral information to us. Of course
it can be mistaken as such, and it is misunderstood if we say
that this is no 'neutral information' for faith; that faith must hold
fast to the assertion of the resurrection. For in that case it holds
fast only to a conception in the history of religion, yet this must
not be identified as such with the 'cause' which concerns us here.
But on the other hand we must admit at once that the significance
of this reflection is its preservative effect. This is due to the fact
that it makes possible a further function. This can also be expressed
by saying that the reflection has a significance which *substantiates*.
Now this means that it is intended to provide the reason why
after Good Friday it is still possible and right to commit ourselves
to the 'purpose' of Jesus, that is, because he has indeed been
raised.

But in doing so we must never forget that such a commitment
can certainly take place, even without saying *expressis verbis*: He is

risen. It is thus by no means *necessary* to speak of Jesus' resurrection in just *this* terminology. But it is at the same time evident that we support, that we facilitate the continuance of the function, if the fact of this continuance is substantiated by the interpretation: He has been raised from the dead. Of course at that time people did not realize that to speak of Jesus' resurrection was an outcome of reflection. But when once this had been accomplished, it then formed the new basis for reflection and argument. Now the outcome of the first thoughts were reflected further, a development which can be traced in the whole wide range of christological statements: the *kerygma* of Jesus' words and deeds becomes a *kerygma* of Christ's *person*. This *kerygma* of Christ then forms the starting-point from which further reflection proceeds. This happens then throughout in such a way that we lose sight of the origin of the earlier *kerygma* of Christ (arising out of his words and deeds). Today the christological 'change' is usually expressed by saying that the preacher becomes the subject of the preaching. We might also formulate it thus: the one who brings salvation becomes the subject of salvation. But later on he, too, can be (and only be) the subject of salvation if he *brings* this salvation. The fact that the preacher becomes the subject of the preaching, that he himself is now preached, should not mean that the preacher is presented by himself (in isolation, although there is also no doubt that the development of christology has not infrequently gone astray in this direction). But this preaching of the preacher must always at *the same time* set out to *bring* what the preacher (who was not yet identified) had brought (previously). That Jesus is the Christ after all only means something, if we are told what this Christ *brings*. Here too it depends decisively on his acts, rather than on his nature. For that can only be inferred from his acts. It is true that, as we have said, this factor of his acts (especially when thinking is carried on further) is often left out of account.

This applies also, to continued reflection on the thought 'he has been raised'. We have already pointed to one association, namely, that at the end of time the raising of the dead to life is expected. If it is said: Jesus *has been* raised, something is asserted about *him* which for mankind is otherwise a hope. But in that case, by the raising of Jesus the end has already dawned. With his raising from the dead the last day *has* already begun and in this way 'the raising of Jesus' *becomes* the central date of 'salvation-history'.

Reflection can also be carried on in another manner. We need to consider in what relation the raising of Jesus from the dead stands to the raising of the dead in general. It is too easily forgotten that the raising of the dead is a conception in the history of religion, but by no means a specifically Christian one. By more or less ignoring the background, or by actually cutting it off from this conception, the resurrection of the dead (or only the resurrection of Christians) is apparently substantiated quite anew by Jesus' resurrection which becomes (without much thought and too little discrimination) the ground of the hope for the future in general. In that case the resurrection-body may also become the subject of reflection, and so on.

Indeed that already occurred in the New Testament, and in this connexion attention may be drawn at least briefly to a problem which in our complicated group of questions it is always worth including in our considerations. Hope for the future is by no means always a hope for resurrection. It can even happen that on account of the hope for the future the expectation of the resurrection is explicitly rejected. This seems to have been the case in Corinth where vicarious baptism was practised (I Cor. 15.29), which of course has no meaning unless the dead are expected to have a future, but where it was nevertheless asserted that there is no resurrection of the dead (I Cor. 15.12).

This can only be understood if we pay attention to the particular form of the anthropology prevailing there, which (especially in the Greek-Hellenistic area) is dualistic. The self (or the soul) is contrasted with the body which is understood as the prison of the self. At the death of the body the self (released at last from prison) leaves the body and acquires a future. How this is gained (by initiation, sacraments or by gnosis) need not be discussed here. But we can understand that for people with this anthropological conception the hope of resurrection is far from being the object of endeavour. For it would mean for them that they would now again have to carry with them the body from which they had just hoped to be released.

It may be instructive (at least from the point of view of methodology) if we consider (of course hypothetically) what thoughts would have been aroused by the incident of Jesus being seen if the witnesses had had this anthropological conception. They would then perhaps have said: Jesus himself (and that means in fact Jesus) did not remain dead together with his body. Jesus is at last released from prison; the prison has died, but Jesus lives! This is what we have come to know. It would then have been said: In Jesus himself (= Jesus) the hope for the future has already been realized. And of course that would then have meant for these people something real; it would not in the least have been understood as a 'spiritualization'. It would have been said that Jesus had *really* left his body, and that the presupposition for this was the fact that he could then be seen. No word would have been said about 'resurrection'.

This is of course only a combining of ideas, but it can at least show us this: If in the Jewish sphere what happened to be seen was interpreted as resurrection, if it was said that this seeing could only occur because Jesus had risen (and then there was naturally also the conviction of Jesus' resurrection), then this is connected with the particular form of *Jewish* anthropology.

Unlike the Greek-Hellenistic anthropology the Jewish anthropology is not dualistic, but monistic. In it man is understood to be a unity, and in that case the future hope must of course be expressed by the conception of resurrection.

Hence the *common* hope for the future makes use at any given time of *different* conceptions, which are based on the anthropology of the time. If this is perceived, it can be recognized at once that it is not permissible to treat as equivalents hope for the future and hope for resurrection (as has frequently been the case without thinking). But this raises the question of *our* anthropology. If we consider our hymns from this point of view we shall find that in a large number of cases the soul is mentioned quite naturally, thus obviously still under the influence of the Greek-Hellenistic anthropology. It can be explained quite simply how this has happened. The hope for the future within the framework of Christian tradition did indeed have its origin in the Jewish sphere of conceptions, but was then modified by the Greek-Hellenistic sphere. The beginning of this blending can be perceived already in I Cor. 15.35ff., for there the 'imperishable' body is described in relation to the terrestrial body as *totaliter aliter*. Here the basis of the early hope of resurrection has already been abandoned, which was particularly interested (from an anthropological point of view) in the identity of the body. But Paul was obliged merely because of his discussion with his opponents to give further thought to their presuppositions, and could not avoid drawing their conceptions into his argument.

But in the present day we simply cannot accept (as happens only too easily) any kind of conceptions about the future as a binding tradition to be taught, if these conceptions are no longer in keeping with the anthropology which actually controls our life. The difficulty of preaching today is to no small extent due to the fact that the philosophical, and particularly the anthropological presuppositions for the earlier affirmations are no longer generally accepted today. At least this difficulty should be perceived, so that the argument does not always concern itself with 'faith' in those matters in which faith does not come into question.

It ought, so it seems to me, to be evident that further reflection carried on so continuously on these lines can easily lead to all kinds of speculations. Such speculations do not after all simply become 'true' in the theological sense, because they were pursued already in New Testament times and then found themselves included in the New Testament. Of course their existence can be confirmed historically, a development of conceptions can be traced; but then the question whether they are theologically justified will also have to be considered.

This is now what remains to be done. However, I shall not enter upon the discussion of the problem of systematic theology, but shall ask if the commentator can offer aids to solve the problem, or whether he can perhaps show where (probably, and consistently with his own work hitherto) the point of departure for the solution of this sytematic problem is to be found.

For this purpose let us start once again from the experience of the appearances. As we saw, it came to be spoken of in two ways, first (by taking action) in such a way that the old 'purpose' was set in motion afresh, second (by reflection) so that fresh contents came into being, in fact by accepting what had been interpreted as 'resurrection' and by continuing to interpret this interpretation further. The question presents itself to us thus (formulated tersely): What is the relationship between the early contents (which had been set in motion afresh by action) and the new contents (which then supervened by reflection)? We can also formulate the problem as follows: *How new* (how *fundamentally new*) is in fact what we are accustomed to denote by the code-word 'Easter'?

The decision about this, in my opinion, must be made after we decide how the conception, 'resurrection of the dead', no doubt already in use, is to be regarded. Two possibilities are conceivable, and they must be discussed in turn.

First, the conception is, so to speak, the *Leit-motiv*, the elucidating background dominating everything; hence the experience of seeing Jesus after his crucifixion must be fitted into this conception. If that proves to be correct, then the way leads from the existing conception to Jesus, so that *he* is now included in it. In that case we might say that this conception has been realized by means of Jesus. Then we would of course also be justified in deducing his resurrection simply from the appearance, for if our attitude is determined by this conception, how should we explain the seeing of a man who was crucified in any other way than as the *consequence* of a raising from the dead which had taken place? And in that case naturally Jesus' resurrection would in fact be the central and therefore the decisive eschatological datum, because from the outset (and not only after Good Friday) resurrection was understood to be the decisive eschatological datum. In the raising of Jesus we should then be concerned with the dawn of the age of eternity—or whatever name we wish to give to this event.

Everything that would otherwise be subsequent reflection would now indeed also be connected with the experience of the seeing by means of reflection, but it would nevertheless be already present (just because it is a *leit-motiv*). In that case, of course, we should have to say that what is Christian is merely a modification of apocalyptic, and the raising of Jesus from the dead would be the apocalyptic expectation realized in fact.

But we must now also look at the consequences which would ensue. The earthly Jesus would be, so to speak, merely the precursor of the Risen One, and all that he preached or did would stand, as it were, in a parenthesis which would disappear only through the resurrection; or (as Wilckens expresses it:) the ministry of Jesus on earth, the claim of the earthly Jesus, needed to be legitimized by eschatology, to be ratified by God.[12] This

---

[12] U. Wilckens, 'Das Offenbarungsverständnis in der Geschichte des Urchristentums', in: *Offenbarung als Geschichte*, ed. W. Pannenberg (1961), pp. 58-63.

was then imparted by God through the resurrection of Jesus. What Jesus did and brought would in that case have been no more than a *prelude*.

It would not, in my opinion, alter the situation if we suppose that Jesus was aware of the part he was playing in this prelude, if we suppose that Jesus saw himself involved in this scheme, that he himself was intent on this divine ratification. Wilckens conjectures that 'Jesus carried the discussions with the Pharisees' theology to extremes, trusting that God would demonstrate by his fate the truth of his claim. In view of the events in Jerusalem Jesus evidently expected God to act eschatologically and finally to endorse his own authority . . .'.[13]

But here we must report most serious misgivings. I am of the opinion that our sources do not enable us to perceive how Jesus understood his death.[14] Even if his journey to Jerusalem had been like a journey to the crisis, yet this does not mean that Jesus forced his death there, as it were, as a prerequisite of a resurrection to come, because only in that case could his claim obtain a ratification at the hand of God. And even if we were willing to concede this (which I certainly consider quite out of the question), then we should still have to say that this concerned the very last stage of his ministry.

In framing these theories we must not simply bypass the question of the sources. Originally the Synoptic material consisted of separate fragments. That applies first to the broad and complicated mass of the material dealing with Jesus' discourses and ministry, but it also applies largely to the material which was later admitted into the story of the Passion. Not until the material had coalesced into a consecutive account does the theme of the Passion in particular find its way backwards. But by now the cross and the resurrection are already theologically established facts. At this time the impression is formed that the road which Jesus takes leads first to the cross and then to the resurrection; but that is a subsequent interpretation, and even Wilckens can only explain the announcements of the Passion as springing out of the post-Easter Christian tradition.[15] But if we eliminate this motif, superimposed only secondarily on the tradition, we see

[13] *Ibid.*, p. 61.
[14] Cf. on this, W. Marxsen, 'Erwägungen zum Problem des verkündigten Kreuzes', *New Testament Studies*, 8 (1961/62), pp. 204ff.
[15] Wilckens, *op. cit.*, p. 60.

that the (original) traditions speak only of Jesus' direct claim to sovereignty, to a ministry which *in itself* raised an eschatological claim, but which did not demand ratification.

In the case of the second possibility it is not the idea of the resurrection which forms a *Leit-motiv* into which Jesus should have been or was in fact fitted. The *Leit-motif* was Jesus himself. He had first been crucified, but then had been seen. Now the concept of the raising of Jesus was merely *one* interpretative theory—and only one among others—by the help of which what had happened was reflected upon and brought to utterance.

This would mean that it is not the resurrection which is the decisive *datum* (after all, in the case of the resurrection it is not quite possible to speak of a *datum* in its real sense) but *Jesus* was the '*datum*', his words and deeds. Jesus was experienced *in his earthly ministry* as an anticipation of the *eschaton*, as a divine event. He was experienced as one who shows the way into faith. He was experienced as the one who anticipated judgment, by declaring that men's attitude to himself and to his summons was binding for the end, and therefore final, and in this very way he relieved men of the fear of judgment and showed them a future. Jesus was experienced as one who called sinners and tax collectors to his table and anticipated the eschatological feast here with them, and particularly with those who in themselves (as the Jews thought) did not in the least 'belong'. Jesus was experienced as the one who brought the distant God near, who made the God of the future to be present today, or in whatever manner we wish to express the wealth of imagery, sayings, happenings, conceptions which we find in the synoptic material. This divine event, bound up with him, which was finished once he was dead, was brought into being once again by the fact that he had been seen.

It seems to me that, according to all that I have tried to demonstrate, only the second of the two possibilities mentioned deserves consideration. This is shown first of all by the functional interpretation of the experience of the appearances. The synoptic tradition shows it too in its own way, but equally clearly it is simply misunderstood if it is inserted into the bracket of what is provisional, if we speak of a necessary ratification of Jesus' claim. The original documents simply will not allow this.

We must therefore hold firmly to the fact that the raising of Jesus is not the fundamental *datum* of Christianity. But in that case, how can we explain Paul's proposition: If Christ had not been raised, there would be no 'Church'?

Of course the proposition remains correct. Only it must not be understood to mean that, if Jesus had not been raised from the dead, the Church would have no foundation. The foundation rests on Jesus, on what he did. Nevertheless, unless Jesus had been seen after his crucifixion, the point would never have been reached (so far as we can penetrate into this) when Jesus' 'purpose' would have continued to develop as *his* purpose. To that extent this event is in historical terms fundamental for the Church. We must, if this is true, formulate this still more precisely. If we consult the sources about the fundamental reason for the continuing development of Jesus' 'purpose' and thus for the Church, then *they* give us as the reason that the appearance was experienced. But that set in motion a movement which I have always denoted (formally) as the continuing development of the 'purpose' of Jesus; but this must by no means be understood so thoughtlessly as though it meant 'we will just go on'.

No: The whole richness of the anticipation of the *eschaton* which had taken place by means of and in Jesus now takes place by means of the Church, and in her. She now stands where Jesus stood. She summons and offers future salvation *now*. The primitive community knows itself to be endowed as though with the spirit, expects the Lord who will soon return, prepares itself for his coming, anticipates the judgment by practising forgiveness of sins itself. And precisely it is in this, in its own function, that it becomes aware of the presence of Jesus. For it is not the Christian community itself who is acting, but in what it does and preaches, Jesus is alive with fullness of power, with a claim and, with a promise.

Now the fact that the raising from the dead occurred is not really fundamental, for to speak in such a way is after all *to turn into history what was the result of an interpretation*. This was no doubt *intelligible*, perhaps even necessary at that time, but it is *forbidden* to us in the present day.

Christian theology therefore cannot and may not on any account *start* from Jesus' resurrection; it cannot argue from it as its *ostensible centre*; on the contrary, the precise opposite is true. We must *inquire* with what objective basis it is permissible to speak at all in Christian terms of the resurrection of Jesus.

This brings before us once again the parallel with the problem of the development of christology (the proclaimer becomes the one who is proclaimed). In virtue of Jesus' act as the Saviour he is later declared to be the *deliverer* of salvation. This then happens on the one hand by the transfer to him of titles (Messiah, Saviour, Son of God, finally: God), on the other hand by designating certain data of his life (birth, death on the cross) as data of salvation. The preaching of Jesus' acts becomes the preaching of Christ's person. Here, concepts and ideas which are well known in the world round about, and thus are readily available, are transferred to him. And that is why here too the question must always be raised: By what right does this happen? All these designations are legitimate, insofar as they create correct terms for the salvation brought by Jesus, and make possible the fresh release of an act, the occurrence of *the same* salvation. All these (personal) interpretative theories concerning Jesus and the emphasis on the data of his life must not be made objective, but must always remain interpretative theories (belonging to their own period). As such they do not supplement each other but stand side by side completely equal in importance. They keep their rights *if* (and always only *insofar* as) they enable Jesus' purpose to be made known later on, and thereby to come to pass.

Analogous statements apply to the interpretative statement, namely, 'Jesus is risen'. We have shown that the earthly Jesus, by what he did already in his earthly ministry, faced men with the God to come and thereby anticipated the future, and within the framework of apocalyptic thought Jesus' 'resurrection' signifies that an event, expected in itself to be in the future, had already taken place *in him*; if these statements are true then it becomes evident that here too the *acts* of the earthly Jesus are affirmed of his *person* when he is designated as the Risen One. Thus the *kerygma* of Jesus (dealing with his acts) reinforced by the result of an apocalyptic interpretation was declared to be a *kerygma* of Christ (dealing with his person).

This interpretative theory, too, must not be objectified; it must remain as an interpretative theory. But it retains (like the other theories of interpretation) its rights, its theological legitimacy, *if* (and always only *insofar* as) it is able to make known Jesus' purpose. But that is what it does, as we have shown. For it is able to make Jesus' purpose known just because it declares him to be the one who, when on earth, anticipated the *eschaton* and thereby ushered in the last days.

Thus the question of the resurrection of Jesus is not that of an event which occurred after Good Friday, but that of the earthly Jesus, and the question, inseparably linked with it, of how this purpose later became a reality of experience which can still be experienced today.

Therefore we may not, and must not, concentrate our attention on the wrong point. It is by no means the case that the appearance which those men saw, still less their interpretation of this appearance as the resurrection of Jesus, guarantees the truth of the message. The problem of truth never presents itself to us unrelated to the message directed at us, and this message, if it is delivered in suitable terms, affirms and promises to us in the present day the words and deeds of the earthly Jesus.

But if I then today in a sermon am touched by his *kerygma* it thus meets me as coming from 'flesh and blood' in human words. But if the Father in heaven opens my heart, then a reality discloses itself to me which is more complex than what the word of man imparts. Then the *eschaton* is anticipated for me.

Here then I encounter Jesus' offer. But when it really touches me, then I know that he is alive. And if I wish to express this in the earlier terminology (and am aware of the limitations within which affirmation in that terminology can be made) then I can confess *today* that he is alive, that he was not held in death. He is risen.

Ulrich Wilckens

THE TRADITION-HISTORY OF THE RESURRECTION OF JESUS

THE whole of the New Testament shares the simple conviction that Jesus passed from the death, which he died upon the cross, to new and eternal life with God in heaven above, where he is now enthroned in glory, and from whence he will shortly appear at the end of the age. The wording of this sentence has deliberately been chosen to express the essential agreement of all the New Testament witnesses, and at the same time to take account of the differences in their statements. Thus, for example, when Paul speaks of Jesus being raised by the act of God in raising him, he is not saying exactly the same as the tradition of the Marcan prophecies of the suffering and resurrection of Jesus, which speak of the resurrection of the Son of Man as his own act (Mark 8.31; 9.31; 10.34). The Fourth Evangelist in fact makes Jesus speak of his 'going' to the Father. Again, the Epistle to the Hebrews does not explicitly mention the resurrection of Jesus (cf., however, 13.20), and speaks only of the ascension of the Son and high priest to the heavenly sanctuary, where he has 'sat down at the right hand of the Majesty on high' (Heb. 1.3; cf. 4.14; 8.1f.; 9.24; 10.12f.; 12.2). But every passage has in view the same event, by which Jesus who was dead passed into divine *life*. In fact the whole New Testament is united in what it says about this event, which indeed in all the New Testament writings forms part of what is *fundamental* to Christian life and to faith in Jesus Christ. Paul reflects this common basic tradition when he says (I Cor. 15.12ff.) that without this event there could not be any faith in Jesus Christ, and therefore there could not be salvation for those who believe in him. Admittedly, this event is not the sole and exclusive basis of New Testament Christianity. What is said about this event in its turn implies certain assumptions, without which it would not take the form in which it is affirmed in primitive Christianity. These assumptions are principally those of the existence and rule of God, that is, of course, the God of Israel, the creator of the universe and the ruler of all its destiny, from the beginning to the end of the ages, God who sent forth the Old Testament prophets and who is the Father of Jesus—in short, everything primitive Christianity has to say about *God*. This is not restricted in its scope to the discussion of the death and resurrection of Jesus, but goes beyond it, and forms its basis and underlying assumption. The same is true, in a different way, of what is said of man and human sin. But however important it may be to take into account this factor in the New Testament understanding of the resurrection of Jesus, it is equally important to recognize that the resurrection of Jesus is as it were the focus of everything proclaimed in the New Testament, including its statements about God and man. To quote the typical testimony of Paul once again, if the resurrection of Jesus had not taken place, God would certainly exist, but only as the God of the wrath to come at the end of time (cf. I Thess. 1.10). Men would still exist, but as sinners who face the wrath of God in the final age (cf. I Cor. 15.17). Thus there could not be what is essential to Christianity as such, the doctrine of God's *salvation* for men (cf. I Cor. 15.19). This is dependent upon the event of the resurrection of Jesus (if I may use this term, with the qualifications noted above, as a general term for the event by which Jesus came to life).

Similarly, in the Church this New Testament conviction is fundamental to the whole Christian tradition. There has never been any Christian life which did not assume the fundamental significance for salvation of the resurrection of Jesus. Until the eighteenth century this assumption was never contested as such. But since that time it has begun to be questioned, so that it has become necessary to inquire into its truth and meaning. Since that time, so far as questions are asked about Christianity at all, inquiry has been made into the truth of belief in the resurrection in two respects. First, there has been a *critical historical* inquiry into what can be concluded from the New Testament texts, as documents of the history of primitive Christianity, about the meaning of the statements on the subject in those texts, and about what really happened in the events of the resurrection. Secondly, the *critical and systematic* question of the reality and truth of the gospel of the resurrection for us at the present day, and for our experience and understanding, has also been posed. The critical element in such questions is something that has long been unavoidable; as theologians, with no choice whether we inquire critically or uncritically into the resurrection of Jesus Christ, we must accept the point of view imposed on us by our past; we must take up, subject to fresh examination and hand on in a new form the previous achievements of critical study. It is important to bear this constantly in mind, in order to resist the absurd idea that scientific criticism can either destroy the substance of the living experience of Christianity, or is capable on the other hand of placing it for the first time on a proper basis. It is both more and less than this. It is the offspring of modern Christianity itself, forms a necessary part of it, and is not like a tool at the Church's disposal, which can be thrown away or curbed if it does the Church any damage. On the other hand, theological criticism is in no sense the whole of Christianity. Nor does it come at the beginning of Christianity, but rather as it were at the end. It presupposes the existence of Christianity as a whole in its present form, and its own task is to reflect upon it 'retrospectively'. Of course this critical work forms part of the present day life of Christianity, in the sense, moreover, of 'an activity which guides the Church' (Schleiermacher).[1] It produces effects upon Christianity, and these effects form an essential part of the life of the Reformation churches, but they never determine the whole of that life (which is often to the advantage of the Church!); for scientific theology is of its essential nature only *one* of the many ways in which the Christian Church lives, and nourishes the life committed to it.

The purpose of these general introductory remarks is to define the task undertaken in this essay. They are intended to show that it is advisable to keep within reasonable bounds our expectations and fears—for example, that the good or ill of our Church may be completely dependent on our theological work and discussion, that the common study of a Theological Commission could actually produce on behalf of the Church a definitive statement for contemporary preaching on the level of a credal confession, or that it is a bad sign if it should prove incapable of this. A con-

[1] F. Schleiermacher, *Kurze Darstellung des theologischen Studiums zum Behuf einleitender Vorlesungen*, ed. H. Scholz, 4th ed. §3.

siderable measure of almost frivolous liberty must be accorded to theological study as the necessary breathing space without which it cannot flourish and cannot fulfil its task in the Church. This is particularly the case where, as with regard to the resurrection of Jesus, which all concede to be a *fundamentally* important element of our Christian tradition of belief, we nevertheless continue to hold different views. Of course any respectable theological assertion has its cutting edge, its specific points of agreement and disagreements with other such assertions. But a theological affirmation or denial cannot meaningfully have the power of binding and loosing, nor is it good for the Church to seek to exalt a theological affirmation or denial to the rank of a confession of faith, except in a clear case of emergency. In general, St Paul's admonition to his congregation in Thessalonica, τὸ πνεῦμα μὴ σβέννυτε (I Thess. 5.19), is true of academic theological debate. This is the case even where the matter under discussion is of fundamental importance.

In what follows, I shall restrict myself to the purely historical aspect of the critical inquiry into the 'significance of the resurrection of Jesus for belief in Jesus Christ'. That is, the question I shall ask is what the New Testament *said* in its historical context; and I shall not ask at the same time what it *says* to us today. Our task here is to look back upon primitive Christianity, and to understand it and make it as widely and clearly accessible as possible. This is only part, a fragment, of the task of answering the questions posed to present day Christians by our terms of reference. But I am of the belief that we are right in our modern tactics of not attempting to solve problems of systematic theology at the same time as we carry out historical study, let alone allowing exegetical work to turn straight away into a sermon. Such diffidence on the part of New Testament exegesis of course makes its general theological range narrower, but perhaps gives it a more profound historical vision and a greater loving concern to do justice to every testimony of primitive Christianity.

The *task* of the historical study of the New Testament testimonies to the resurrection is to describe the distinctive nature of each one, and to discuss the process by which they have come into being, which alone provides an adequate understanding of each individual testimony. Thus its procedure is laid down in advance. First, it must analyse the testimonies and demonstrate their relationship to one another in the history of the tradition; this process must go back to the preliminary stages, and as far as possible to the origins of the history of the tradition. Secondly, and on the basis of this first inquiry, the tradition-history of the whole primitive Christian testimony to the resurrection can be reconstructed. One of the difficulties of this procedure is that the tradition-history of the testimonies to the resurrection cannot really be separated from the whole complex of the tradition-history of primitive Christianity. Consequently, in what follows we shall adopt in our argument many views advanced elsewhere, without attempting to justify them ourselves. At the same time, many aspects of the testimonies of the resurrection which properly belong to our subject will be excluded, without special note being made of the fact.[2]

The same is also true of the brief general summary of the testimonies which we shall now undertake in order to get our bearings. The resurrection is frequently mentioned in the New Testament epistles, but for the most part they contain no reference to the material on the resurrection in the gospel narrative. This remarkable fact is associated with the general observation that in the New Testament epistles, any reference whatsoever to the gospels is extremely rare. The explanation which I would give of this situation is that it is typical of the tradition-history of primitive Christianity in general, for from its origin it follows two distinct courses. The first was the tradition of Jesus which was originally formed and handed down in the circle of the primitive community, from where, however, it found its way into the Syrian diaspora, but not into the missionary churches founded by Paul. Secondly, the tradition of the missionary churches was determined by a *kerygma*, parenesis and liturgy of a quite distinctive structure, which probably goes back to the circle of those who are known as 'Hellenists', who for a short time existed independently in Jerusalem, and then set up centres of their own in the diaspora, from which further missions were sent out. Throughout this circle virtually nothing was preached or known about the teaching

[2] I should like to emphasize that this essay was prepared for a particular discussion and was read there, and at the request of the Theological Commission of the Evangelical Union Church was printed unaltered in its present form, and does not satisfy every requirement proper to academic publications. But I hope that in the not too distant future I may present what I read there in a more adequately based form.

and acts of Jesus for a long time, but only about his death, his resurrection, and his function as saviour and judge in the last days. On the basis of this primitive *kerygma*, the outline of which can be seen, for example, in I Thess. 1.9f., an independent 'theology' was formed. It was understandably subject to powerful influence from Hellenistic concepts and ideas. For example, a cosmic christology was developed, as we can see in particular from the liturgical hymns which we possess from this area of tradition. They sing of the pre-existence of the Son of God with the creator of the universe, his function as a universal cosmic mediator, his descent to earth among men, his humiliation, death and exaltation, and his investment with the office of a universal cosmic ruler (cf. Phil. 2.5-11; Col. 1.15-20, also Rom. 1.3f. as Paul understands it). Paul makes particularly frequent use of this 'theology of exaltation' (cf. e.g. II Cor. 8.9), and it underlies the theological treatise of the Epistle to the Hebrews in its entirety.

The development of christology in the group centering on the primitive congregation, where the tradition of the gospel material was formed, was quite different. It is particularly significant that there the whole of christology found its expression in the portrayal of Jesus before the events of the resurrection, and this is true even of later christologies (including that of the Gospel of John). To a limited extent the authors of the written gospels (at least the authors of the Gospels of Mark and Luke) began an attempt to reconcile the different 'theologies' of the two independent spheres of tradition. This gospel literature continued to affect Christian tradition-history in the second century. It played an important part in ensuring that the early Catholic Church preserved the gospel tradition at all, in addition to the apostolic tradition, and then accorded it the first place in the present canon, before the epistles.

The hypothesis about the whole course of primitive Christian tradition which has been roughly outlined here will not be further discussed in what follows. It will provide the framework in which individual testimonies of the resurrection are analysed, which we shall now proceed to do.

It has become customary to begin with the testimony to the resurrection which is the oldest in the *literary* sense, I Cor. 15.3ff. But we must warn against allowing our judgment on the whole of the history of the tradition to be influenced by the history of literary material, to an extent greater than the latter permits, as though this *text*, which is the oldest we possess, represented the earliest stage of the tradition, and as though the testimonies to the resurrection in the gospel, which are unquestionably more recent in the literary sense, should be judged on the basis of I Cor. 15. It is better to evaluate this passage in the first instance as a fundamental testimony from the sphere of tradition represented by the Pauline missionary churches.

It is generally agreed today that this passage—at least in I Cor. 15.3-5—contains material from a kerygmatic and catechetical tradition which had a fixed form before Paul made use of it. Because the wording of the Greek is close to that of a Semitic language, it has frequently been suspected, with good reason, that an Aramaic or Hebrew original lies behind the existing text. This in itself, of course, is no reason for supposing that it arose in the circle of tradition formed by the primitive community in Jerusalem; for it must be accepted, for example, that the Syrian communities were at least bilingual, so that on this basis the formula could have come into being in Antioch just as well as in Jerusalem.[3] But in any case the formula is very old; if Paul himself had 'received' it (I Cor. 15.3), it follows that it was very probably in use before AD 50 in Antioch, and perhaps even before AD 40 in Damascus, which was Paul's first home community. But this means that it is perfectly possible that this formula was common to the oldest missionary communities of the diaspora and goes back to the circle of the 'Hellenists', who in their turn (whatever the wording may have been) learned it from the primitive community.

What does this formula say? In four lines it speaks of the death, burial, raising and appearances of 'the Christ'. (1) The statement concerning the death of Christ has been analysed by Marxsen, and in essentials I agree with him.[4] (2) There is no doubt that ὅτι ἐτάφη (v. 4a) belongs in the context of the statement concerning his death: Jesus died and was buried, the fact of his dying is final. From the point of view of the history of the tradition, this statement perhaps signifies that certain traditions about Jesus'

[3] Hans Conzelmann, 'Zur Analyse der Bekenntnisformel I Kor. 15.3-5', *Ev Th* 25 (1965), pp. 1-11, esp. pp. 5f., argues against any kind of Semitic original for the formula.

[4] This reference is to the manuscript of a lecture which has not yet been published.

grave existed in the place from which the formula originally derived its material. This cannot be excluded in view of the fact that Paul himself obviously has no concrete knowledge about Jesus' grave, nor of the finding of the empty tomb. For what Paul himself, and indeed the group in Antioch from whom he 'received' the formula, did not know, and did not associate with the expression ἐτάφη, *could* have been known and handed down in the primitive community, if the *content* of the Hellenistic Christian formula originally derived from a tradition of the primitive community. However, no certainty can be obtained from I Cor. 15 itself. But I Cor. 15.4a can in no way be regarded, as has frequently been the case, as an argument that at the time of the writing of I Cor. the stories about the burial of Jesus and the finding of his empty tomb, which are recorded in Mark 15 and 16, could not yet have existed as such. (3) The statement in v. 4b concerning his raising is meant in the sense that his raising was something which *was done to* Jesus; the perfect ἐγήγερται signifies God's action upon Jesus in raising him. Κατὰ τὰς γραφάς may be a secondary addition, introduced in order to make v. 4 correspond to v. 3; in any case the scriptural testimony for the raising of Jesus came into being considerably later than that for his passion and death. Finally, the meaning and origin of the expression 'on the third day' is still disputed, and not satisfactorily explained. But it is certain that it is intended to give the date of the event of his raising as such, and not of his first appearance.[5] (4) The mention of his appearances has the same relation to the statement about his raising as the statement about his burial to that about his death: it is intended to confirm his raising, by naming the witnesses of the risen Christ.

Marxsen[6] is not to be followed in giving as the reason why the subject in v. 5 is Χριστός and not ἐγηγερμένος or something similar, the hypothesis that the fact of the resurrection of him who appeared was not an essential presupposition of the function of his appearance for those who witnessed it, so that it is never explicitly mentioned as such. When Paul says ὤφθη κἀμοί it follows unambiguously from the whole context that he whom he too has seen (cf. I Cor. 9.1) is regarded as *he who has risen*, and

---

[5] I disagree here with F. Hahn, *Christologische Hoheitstitel*, 1963, pp. 205f.

[6] 'Die Auferstehung Jesu als historisches und als theologisches Problem', 1964, pp. 13f.; 22; ET, see pp. 22f., 34 above.

whom he has to preach as an apostle like 'the others'. The preaching of the *raising* of Christ as an act of God, exercised upon Jesus who was dead, is confirmed by the appearances, which can be specified, of this Christ. There is no doubt that this is the function of the list of witnesses (vv. 5-8) in the context of the argument in I Cor. 15. Thus we are perfectly justified in speaking of the appearances of the risen Christ.

Of course we are also justified in asking whether the specifying of the appearances in the history of the tradition had from the first the *sole* function of confirming the raising of Jesus by the testimony of those who had seen him as the risen Christ. The context of the three passages in which Paul explicitly mentions what had happened to him show unambiguously that he at least experienced his own *calling* and authorization as an apostle in seeing the risen Christ (cf. I Cor. 9.1; 15.8-10; Gal. 1.12, 15). Since his apostolate involved a special personal mission to preach to the Gentiles, he had an obvious reason for laying special emphasis on his own legitimation as an apostle, by contrast to the generally recognized apostolic authority of those who were called before him (I Cor. 15.8-10). But this permits us to conclude that the others whom he lists in vv. 5-7 thought of and affirmed the appearances which had happened to them as having exactly the same structure as his. This means that as far as we can tell, Paul's understanding can be taken as representative of that which pre-vailed in the Church at his time. To have seen the risen Jesus when he appeared meant for one to whom this had happened not merely that he thereby became a witness to the event of the raising of Jesus, but at the same time that as such a witness he also received special authority within the Church. The appearance of Jesus, the testimony to the raising of Jesus, legitimation as a witness and the commission to preach the risen Jesus clearly formed a single whole in the understanding of the appearance of the risen Jesus.

This is also confirmed by an analysis of the form of the statements concerning the appearances in I Cor. 15.5-7. Harnack frequently and rightly emphasized that the syntactical structure of v. 5 and v. 7 is the same. Whereas v. 6 is clearly formulated by Paul, who is using the traditional story of the appearance to more than five hundred as part of an argument for the purposes of his debate with the Church at Corinth ('most of whom are still alive, though some have fallen asleep'),[7] vv. 5 and 7 are sentences in a fixed form, which Paul probably received with this wording. In each case the name of an individual comes first, and is followed by a group. If one can assume here the interpretation of the appearances described above, this means that both sentences describe a relationship of authority, and what we have here are 'legitimation formulae'.[8] It is sufficient for this purpose simply to specify the fact of the appearance as such—the specification of a person by giving a name constitutes the whole form of these traditional formulae. 'He (Christ) appeared to Cephas, then to the twelve' simultaneously signifies that Peter (Cephas) is the first in the circle of the twelve. The same is true of v. 7: James is first in the circle of all the apostles. Harnack and others after him tried to see in this evidence of a rivalry between Peter and James. This thesis has been widely rejected, and rightly so. But there was something correct in Harnack's observation: the two sentences express the validity of an authority, and are presumably evidence of two different situations in the history of the Church within the primitive community, each of which can be recognized in the Epistle to the Galatians[9] and in the Acts of the Apostles.[10]

If this is correct, then one can be more confident in accepting on the basis of vv. 5 and 7, that the whole tradition in I Cor. 15.3-7 has its origin in the primitive community or close to it. But this analysis in fact leads to the conclusion that we can isolate here an ancient, and in part the most ancient, tradition of the resurrection. V. 5 at least asserts an event which, according to all our information, resulted in the constituting of the primitive community after the resurrection. The appearance to Peter was the first appearance to take place. It was followed by a similar event which happened to a group of the twelve; and from stories which have not taken on a fixed form, Paul knows of a further appearance to a large group of persons known by name—which presumably was simply the group of the primitive community which formed on the basis of the experience undergone by Peter and the twelve.

---

[7] Cf. I Cor. 15.12ff. and I Thess. 4.13ff.

[8] Cf. the discussions in *Dogma and Denkstrukturen, Festschrift for E. Schlink*, 1963, pp. 63ff.

[9] Cf. Gal. 2.9 on the one hand with 1.18f., and on the other hand with 2.11f.

[10] Cf. Acts 2.14; 3.1ff.; 5.1ff., 29ff.; 8.14ff.; 12.1ff. with 9.32ff.; 10.1ff.; 15.6ff.; 21.15ff.

'Veterans' are known by name, because they are honoured as elders; in Acts 6.5 and 13.1 we possess examples of this from other communities.

Thus if I Cor. 15.5ff. gives us, with great probability, an insight into the earliest origins of the history of the Church, we are then faced with the question of how in fact the appearances which were vouchsafed at the beginning to Peter and the twelve could lead to the certainty that Jesus had been raised. If in general terms the appearances were the sole means by which this certainty, on which the Church was founded, came into being, how was it possible, what was the reason, and what factors were at work, for these experiences to have had such an effect?

I am in entire agreement with Marxsen[11] and others, that it is not methodologically permissible to deny that this question belongs to the province of the historian as such, and to reserve it to the realm of pure matters of faith. Of course an historical investigation can never give a wholly adequate explanation of the coming into being of new and effective factors in history, because the arbitrary element, which is part of the nature of such newly occurring events, is not susceptible to the process of analogical comparison which is the basic methodological principle of all historical investigation. But there is never anything *wholly* contingent in history; and this is also true of the appearances of the risen Jesus. Even if we were to follow earlier scholars, belonging to a period of scholarship now superseded, and saw them as taking place solely within the individual souls of the disciples who received them, and sought to explain them as sudden emotional change or the like, we would have to demonstrate that such a thing was *possible*. And precisely because it is quite impossible that disciples of Jesus should have reacted to the catastrophes of his death by the conviction suddenly dawning upon them that he had been raised from the dead—which had never previously been asserted in Israel of any mortal—the so-called hypothesis of the subjective vision must be excluded as an explanation.

If we now analyse the conceptions which the earliest bearers of the tradition of the appearances associated with the appearances of the risen Jesus to which they bore witness, there are three assumptions which are of essential importance here. I give them in the order of their practical importance. The first assumption

[11] Marxsen *op. cit.*, p. 7, cf. p. 19 above.

consists of the concrete events which took place when the disciples were in the company of Jesus. For what was decisive in
what happened in the appearances was that the disciples *recognized*
Jesus, their rabbi, in the one who appeared to them. What is of
importance, of course, is not simply the element of mere recogni-
tion. Rather, what is the decisive assumption in the preaching of
his raising from the dead is that it was *Jesus* whom they recognized,
as the person he had been in his whole ministry.

What is required at this point is an extensive and detailed
account of the ministry of Jesus. This is not possible in the framework of this communication. I must limit myself to a few
remarks of a general nature. Making a unique claim to be giving
the judgment of God in the last days, Jesus himself promised the
kingdom of God—an entity known throughout Jewish tradition
—to every person as valid for him and given to him, with the
explicit inclusion of sinners. He took it upon himself to proclaim
the kingdom of God which was *to come* in the last days, as unequivocally *near*, and as wholly determining the concrete present
moment here and now, in a way which was possible and permissible, by the standards of Jewish tradition, only for God himself.
Consequently it was in fact impossible for him to draw upon any
tradition, as it were, to 'cover' this unparalleled claim; what the
law of the fathers said was not the court of appeal before which
he sought his legitimation—on the contrary, he sometimes spoke
against them. If the tradition is to be relied upon, he made no
appeal—at least no decisive appeal—to any inspiration. Priestly
tradition is completely absent from his sayings. He went over the
heads of the existing authorities and in an unheard-of way simply
claimed the authority of God for his ministry: and yet he was not
God himself! Yet he did not surround himself with any blaze of
glory. Not only did he not claim for himself any of the honorific
titles which were later given him; it is also particularly striking
that the person of Jesus himself is not in any way the theme of
any of his genuine sayings. And yet Jesus frequently speaks in the
first person. It is Jesus who speaks, teaches and acts. And this
Jesus—who appeared on the scene as nothing more than Jesus the
Nazarene—claimed in this comprehensive, compelling and above
all simple and straightforward way, that the final action of *God* in
the last days was to be found in his *own* acts—in such a way as to
suggest that it was natural that he could rightfully make such a

claim. I agree with Marxsen,[12] that if one examines the preaching
of Jesus, no element is visible in it which in any way limits the
all-embracing validity of this authority, which he claims so
straightforwardly, or characterizes it as anything anticipatory.
This can be seen from the often quoted saying concerning the Son
of man in Luke 12.8f.; for it does not make a decision of Jesus at
the present moment dependent upon the decision of the Son of
man in the last days in the future, but precisely the reverse. Thus
the saying is *a promise*: anyone who acknowledges me, the Son of
man *will* acknowledge (that is, not the Son of man will then, for
the first time, have to confirm the acknowledgment of me, but
that the Son of man *will* confirm it). And yet, against the view of
Marxsen, I believe that the whole ministry of Jesus is misunderstood—with particular regard to this simple, confident, automatic
and unemphatic assertion of an authority distinct from his own
person—if for all its uniqueness it is not understood on the basis
of the historical form in which the Israelite and Jewish faith in
God was lived. Like every Jew, Jesus assumed that God was the
Creator, had given the law, and would exercise the final decision
concerning salvation and damnation. But with this he also
assumed with regard to his work the fundamental Israelite
realization, without which no devout Jew would have followed
him as a disciple, that no man can claim that God acts in his acts,
if God does not will it. The will of God is *above* Jesus and his acts.
But according to the Jewish conception the will of God is an
effective will; it will be ultimately manifested in the last judgment.
The last judgment, and the events which finally bring it about,
were for every Jew at that time the ultimate criterion for a true or
false claim to have the authority of God. But this must not be
seen in isolation; the eschatological aspect in fact merely makes
more profound what was held in general and fundamentally
concerning God and man and heaven and earth: that the will of
God is the ultimate force of reality. No man—not even Jesus—
can be identical with God: rather, anyone who claims the
authority of God, unless he is presumptuous, assumes thereby a
distinction between himself and God, between his acts and God.
For this reason Jesus did not speak of himself, but of the kingdom
of God, its gift and demands, and so it was left to God to demonstrate the truth of Jesus' claim to possess his authority. When

[12] *Ibid.*, p. 31f.; cf. pp. 45f. above.

Jesus cries, 'Blessed are you poor, for yours is the kingdom of God', this call and the assertion it contains are *Jesus'* affair, for which he himself is responsible, but the realization of his promise is entirely *God's* affair: and the Beatitudes which follow show that —regardless of the present *validity* of the kingdom of God for those he is addressing—it is thought of as a future event in the last days.

Thus the real and actual presence of Jesus was a guarantee to his disciples that God would bring to reality what he had preached. This is the meaning of following Jesus, the only terms in which Jesus made himself a prominent theme of his teaching. To follow *him* means to be drawn into contact with the *kingdom of God* in the sense which it had in his preaching. Consequently, his shameful end during the Passover feast in Jerusalem was a disaster which cannot be overestimated for the discipleship of his disciples. Not only was the actual self-authentication of Jesus now absent—it was even called into question. Could the disciples have put themselves in Jesus' place after his death, come forward as his followers to be the guarantors in themselves of the truth of the kingdom of God in Jesus' sense of the word, and given an answer themselves to the question which since his execution had been raised with regard to everything he had said and done, the question whether his death was not in fact a divine judgment upon him? 'Cursed be everyone who hangs on a tree'; the judgment of the Jewish leaders implied that this saying in the *torah* applied to the shameful death of Jesus of Nazareth.

It is very important to understand that there was no legal basis available to the disciples of Jesus to which they could turn, in order simply to take the place of Jesus after his death. There was no way in which the tradition of the law could be drawn upon to provide this, since Jesus ignored it as authority for his preaching. But even the preaching of Jesus himself, the sayings of Jesus which they remembered, was capable neither of demonstrating that he had been in the right, in spite of the disaster that had overtaken him, nor of justifying his disciples in taking over his preaching as such, on their own authority, without its being 'covered' by Jesus who had preached it. Only the judge of the last days could now utter the last word as to whether Jesus had been right or wrong. If this were true in general, it could likewise only be God himself who was now able to confirm that the former disciples of Jesus had been right to follow him. Without such an authentication of Jesus by God himself, the possibility of discipleship no longer existed. And the practical reaction of the disciples, which seems most probable in spite of the different objections of Marxsen and Campenhausen, their return to their homes in Galilee, is an eloquent expression of the disaster which in practice his death signified for their position within the Israel of that time.

By seeing Jesus, probably there in Galilee, Peter and the twelve experienced the overcoming of this catastrophe by God himself, the reconstituting of the discipleship of Jesus, and the giving to them of a commission to carry on the preaching of Jesus themselves. To use Marxsen's words: 'The whole richness of the anticipation of the *eschaton* which had taken place by means of and in Jesus now takes place by means of the Church, and in her.'[13] How did this come about through the appearances which happened?

Here we come to the second assumption. On the basis of the appearances, the disciples were able to say that Jesus had been raised, because they assumed *the tradition of the Jewish hope of the resurrection*. If we fail to understand this, we fail to understand the meaning of the primitive Christian gospel of *Jesus'* resurrection. At this point all the Jewish testimonies ought to be cautiously studied, both individually and in their mutual relationship in the history of their several traditions. There is on the whole not a great deal of extant material, and the few examples that exist are in part very different from each other. They begin with the Apocalypse of Isaiah, and go on through the Book of Daniel to the Apocalypses of Baruch and Ezra. But they show common features in their conceptual structure. A brief summary of this is as follows. Resurrection is always an act of God in the context of the events of the last days. No one other than God can raise the dead. Resurrection means that God calls the souls or spirits of the dead, lying in the sleep of death in their chambers, from their 'cells' and brings them to himself in the exaltation of his throne of judgment. Thus resurrection is the means by which the dead are carried into the moment of the conclusion of time, in order to receive their final destiny through the judgment of God, whether it be damnation or the salvation of eternal life. Thus resurrection is only resurrection to *life* where God's judgment allots them to

[13] *Ibid.*, p. 34, cf. p. 48 above.

eschatological life; resurrection *can* also be resurrection to eternal damnation. Resurrection is always *initium finis*; that is, it signifies being carried and lifted up to receive a final decision about the destiny of those who are resurrected.

Thus when the disciples saw, in the appearances which they underwent, Jesus, their rabbi, coming from above and restored to life, this meant for them that Jesus had already been carried by God's act of resurrection into the eschatological reality of life which God keeps hidden in heaven. In Marxsen's very formal language,[14] one can say: the statement 'Jesus is risen' is an 'interpretative statement'. The Jewish hope of the resurrection which they brought with them when they experienced the appearance 'interpreted' to them what they saw in the appearance. It is now clear that this interpretative phrase 'raised from the dead' was not arbitrarily chosen, but in the framework of the Jewish eschatological expectation which the disciples shared, was appropriate to what had happened to Jesus, for the knowledge of which the experience of the appearance of the risen Christ was sufficient, as the disciples understood it. For on the basis of the appearance they proclaimed: 'Jesus *has been raised* from the dead.' The knowledge of this *event* is the purpose of the appearance of *Jesus*. For it provided for them the *basis* of the knowledge that Jesus' preaching had *therefore*, by this act of God, already received its final authentication. *As a consequence* they themselves had the right to go on preaching his gospel, and at the same time, in the context of the same appearance, had explicitly received their own commission. *But the essential significance of the raising of Jesus was that it was the eschatological confirmation of the authority or truth of the preaching of Jesus.*

We are now for the first time able to appreciate the two consequences of the experience of the resurrection of Jesus for the history of tradition. First, the primitive community primarily and principally continued to teach and preach *what Jesus himself had taught and preached*, and not in their own name, but solely, and in such a way as to define the form of their preaching, in the name of Jesus himself. Secondly, in this process of tradition the portrait of Jesus before the resurrection became more and more strongly and extensively influenced by that of the eschatologically authenticated preacher of the kingdom of God, so that a specifically post-

14 *Ibid.*, p. 17, cf. p. 28 above.

resurrection christology was formed. To use somewhat over-emphatic terms, the dominant concern of the earliest preaching of the resurrection of Jesus was not that Jesus who had died had come to life, but that Jesus, the preacher of the kingdom of God who had died, had now had his preaching eschatologically authenticated, and had therefore become the standard of judgment for eschatological salvation and damnation, as he had in fact claimed to be in his whole ministry.

But we must now go on to the third assumption. For it is necessary to ask how far the knowledge of Jesus' resurrection is really due to his *appearance* as such? Why was the experience undergone by the disciples known as an 'appearance'? Clearly this experience also possessed a certain 'authority' in itself, since it had the *function* of imparting the knowledge of the resurrection. One must clearly understand that the raising of the dead was understood as an act of God expected at the end of time, and that therefore what the disciples saw was wholly different from earthly miracles of the restoration to life of those who had died, such as are recounted of Elijah in the Bible and of many of the great rabbis in rabbinic tradition. When the disciples saw the risen Jesus, they saw an *eschatological* reality. The *form* of the experience undergone in an appearance is associated with this. To be able to distinguish it, as far as possible, is of great importance for the whole complex of questions which we are discussing.

Here we must at once confess that in this respect the New Testament material gives us little or no help. It is only Paul who gives a more or less clear account of the form of his own experience in the relevant passages of his epistles. Of course not much can be deduced from the term ὤφθη, which Paul takes over in I Cor. 15 from the conventional formula. It is probably to be understood, on the analogy of the passages in the Septuagint, in a deponent sense: 'the one who appears' comes to encounter the human being. It is 'the one who appears' who acts, the person who receives the appearance is passive, he experiences the appearance. In this sense, such an experience means seeing something which is given to the seer to see. Thus it is wholly in accord with the meaning of ὤφθη, when in I Cor. 9.1, from the point of view of his own experience, Paul says, 'Have I not *seen* Jesus our Lord?' Admittedly, events which vary greatly in form are referred to both in the New Testament and in the Septuagint as appearances:

this is true especially of the appearance of angels and above all to that of the 'man of God' or 'angel of Yahweh'.[15] A clearer picture of the special conception which Paul associates with an 'appearance' is to be found only in Gal. 1.15. Here the same experience is referred to as an ἀποκάλυψις, brought about by God, in which God reveals to Paul 'his son', for him to proclaim him to the heathen. Ὑιός here refers to the exalted Jesus, as it does in I Thess. 1.10 and Rom. 1.3f. (as Paul understands it). Thus the title implies the status of him who is revealed: God shows Jesus *as* his Son. In Jewish tradition, which was largely maintained in the language of primitive Christianity, the concept of a 'revelation' was one which signified something quite specific, that is, the unveiling of what God had hidden from the knowledge of the present age. The 'mysteries' of the eschatological future are veiled in this sense; God still keeps them hidden with him in heaven above, but he *will* 'reveal' them to all men, when the last hour has sounded: this they will then experience, by receiving either damnation or salvation. But God is also capable of 'revealing' *in anticipation* the hidden mysteries of the end of time to a few specially chosen men. This kind of pre-eschatological revelation, eschatological in content, takes place through the experience of a specific form of vision. The men who receive them are astonished to receive a sudden miraculous insight into what is hidden; and usually an audible word of interpretation is added to what is seen, or else the visionary sees an angel who at God's command gives him the interpretation. The form of such 'revelations', as we find them particularly in apocalyptic texts, goes back to the ancient prophetic tradition, and structurally has much in common with it; this can still be seen in the fact that Paul formulates his own experience in Gal. 1.15 by echoing the words of the prophetic vocation visions. But they are distinct from the visions of the prophets, in that what is made accessible by revelation to particular seers is on principle hidden, that is, it is heavenly, eschatological reality.

It now becomes clear what Paul is describing as his experience in Gal. 1.15. In such an act of 'revelation' God showed him Jesus as him who is in heaven above with God—because by raising him God had carried him into this realm of what is eschatological and hidden, and had there given him the function of judge of the

[15] Also in the New Testament, cf. Luke 1.11; 22.43.

faithful, deciding upon their salvation. The vision of Stephen in Acts 7.56 is described in similar terms (albeit in association with the concept of the Son of man as it was accepted in the primitive community), whereas in the accounts of the apparition to Paul at Damascus which are given in the Acts of the Apostles the specific character of the experience as a 'revelation' is somewhat overshadowed by the storyteller's art.

Now it is not certain, but obvious from the historical circumstances, that one may accept that the witnesses mentioned in I Cor. 15.5-7 experienced the appearance of Jesus in a structurally similar form to that described by Paul in Gal. 1.15. This view is supported by the fact that Paul claimed that the appearance had for himself the same legitimizing function as it was claimed to have in the case of those who witnessed before him. If one may accept this—albeit wholly hypothetically—then we have a better and more precise understanding of the experience which first occurred to Peter and to the twelve in Galilee: they saw Jesus in the condition of his eschatological life; and they were able to understand what had happened in this sense, not only (though in the first instance) because it was *Jesus* whom they saw, but also because the *form* of the vision experienced by them in this way was known and familiar to them from the apocalyptic tradition of their Jewish environment, as the experience of hidden eschatological reality revealed by God: not from their own, but probably from traditional experience. The knowledge of this form also contributed to the unequivocal certainty with which the disciples recognized what they had seen, and its significance, and continued to proclaim this knowledge.

These three points show the distinction between what the disciples themselves actually experienced, and what was already assumed in this experience and its interpretation. It is the first point in particular which is disputed by Marxsen.[16] Of course it is an oversimplification and falsification of the situation we are discussing to regard the relationship between Jesus' preaching during his ministry, and his resurrection, as that between a 'prelude' and (this would be the necessary equivalent) the true drama which followed. The purpose of the account of Jesus' preaching given above was to correct this impression. Of course, to exaggerate somewhat, one can say that Jesus was the 'har-

[16] Marxsen, *op. cit.*, pp. 31ff.; cf. pp. 45ff. above.

binger of the Risen Christ', but solely with regard to the *eschato-logical* function of the resurrection. But the essence of this is to authenticate his preaching before the resurrection from the direction of the kingdom of God itself. The authentication of Jesus which took place in the resurrection in its turn illuminates his previous ministry, and the post-resurrection tradition of the primitive community responded to this implication by placing at the centre of its tradition not the resurrection itself, but the portrait of the pre-resurrection Jesus! But as we have said, this portrait was only made possible by the event of the resurrection, and virtually every feature of the traditional post-resurrection portrayal of the pre-resurrection Jesus was quite legitimately determined by the event of the resurrection. Jesus now appears as the preacher of the kingdom of God who has *already been* authenticated by the kingdom of God itself, and who as the Son of man who has come from heaven actually possesses in himself the authority of God. Thus the nature of the portrait given of Jesus, which, for example, dominates entirely the stratum of tradition which is the source of the sayings of Jesus, is formed entirely by the *event* of *Jesus'* resurrection. Consequently I must affirm, against Marxsen, the thesis that what is at issue is the event of the resurrection of Jesus itself, and what according to Marxsen is the direct and true sense of the primitive Christian proclamation of the resurrection, the continuation of Jesus' 'purpose', must be regarded as the effect of the resurrection. For the proclamation of the resurrection on the basis of the first appearances of the risen Jesus is not concerned solely with the fact that Jesus *has returned*, but with the fact that Jesus has been *authenticated by God himself*; not that 'he still comes today',[17] but that 'God has raised him and therefore finally justified him'. Consequently, it is not in accordance with the understanding of the resurrection in the primitive community to say that 'Jesus rose into the *kerygma*', neither in Bultmann's sense of this expression, nor in the sense in which Marxsen accepts it.[18] In the sense of the earliest primitive Christian preaching of the resurrection it must be rephrased: 'Jesus rose into the final judgment of God.' *This* event is the whole basis both of the proclaiming of the tradition of Jesus in the primitive community, and also of the Hellenistic Christian missionary *kerygma*.

[17] *Ibid.*, p. 26; cf. p. 39 above.   [18] *Ibid.*, p. 27; cf. p. 40 above.

This is a brief summary of the result of our analysis in terms of tradition-history of the tradition of the appearances. But we have only looked at a part of the source material, working back from I Cor. 15, that is, from the sphere of tradition represented by the missionary churches, and inquiry into the historical origins of this tradition. We must now examine in a similar way the resurrection tradition of the gospels. For reasons of space we cannot afford to discuss it at the same length. The analysis and comparison of the resurrection material in the gospels leads to the following conclusions. (1) The oldest testimony, not merely in the literary sense, but also from the point of view of the history of tradition, is the account in Mark 16.1-8. Here only v. 8b—'and they said nothing to anyone, for they were afraid'—must be excluded as a Marcan redactional addition, associated with the Marcan theory of the messianic secret. Again, the admonition by the angel to the disciples in v. 7 does not form part of the original substance of the passage. Here is the very first evidence of the tendency of the tradition to bring into a narrative unity what happened at Jesus' tomb, and the Galilean appearances of Jesus. The two complexes of tradition, therefore, were originally separate, and were handed down without any explicit connexion with one another. It is also perhaps possible to exclude some phrases from the beginning of the passage as secondary additions. But the body of it is not merely pre-Marcan, but goes back to a very early stage in the history of the tradition. In spite of many opinions to the contrary, I myself consider that it belongs to an early stratum of the passion narrative. This was the context in which it was originally handed down. It was probably never an isolated story. The widespread view that it replaced at a relatively late period an earlier conclusion of the narrative which recounted the appearance to Peter seems to me particularly unconvincing. The passage is rather the earlier conclusion of the passion narrative, taking it on to the resurrection. (2) The story of the empty tomb was elaborated at various stages of the history of the tradition, and in different ways, into a separate and distinct narrative. A pre-Lucan tradition, which was supported by a pre-Johannine tradition, told how the women ran to the disciples, who are here assumed to be in Jerusalem, and how of these Peter ran to the tomb to convince himself (Luke 24.12; cf. John 20.3ff.). Another tradition gives a quite different account of what happened at Jesus' tomb, in which the Jewish leaders are made the principal figures in the action (Matt. 27.62-66; 28.2-4, 11-15). In these various elaborations of the original passage the dominant intention is either to emphasize the reality of the empty tomb as a proof of the resurrection, or to connect the story of the women with the disciples. But right on into the late apocryphal tradition it is clearly evident that the original lack of connexion between the story of the tomb and the traditions of the appearances is maintained.[19]

This observation can be explained with some degree of probability as follows. The primitive community began at a very early period to develop a coherent narrative of Jesus' passion. The significance of the lack of any connexion between the Q stratum of tradition and that of the passion narrative is probably not that the two complexes were handed down by different persons,[20] but that their lack of connexion reveals a different *Sitz im Leben*. The tradition of Jesus' *logia* was as it were the *halacha*, the practical instruction of the primitive community. The *Sitz im Leben* of the passion narrative, on the other hand, was very probably the cult, for the form it takes, that of a coherent narrative divided into pericopes, leads to the conclusion that the purpose of this tradition was not any kind of missionary preaching, nor doctrinal teaching, the give and take of a doctrinal dialogue on the analogy of the method of teaching used in the synagogue, but that of recitation in the context of a cultic memorial of the passion. Now it is unlikely that a narrative of the passion alone would have been handed down; texts such as the summaries which may be supposed to have provided the earlier stages of the so-called prophecies of the passion and resurrection of Jesus, Mark 8.31; 9.31; 10.33f., and similar passages, provide a powerful argument to the contrary. Rather, the narrative of the passion recited in the cult would have concluded with the resurrection, and in fact with the pericope concerning the empty tomb. Why would it have concluded with so indirect a testimony to the resurrection? First, the proclamation by the angel in Mark 16.6 is an important statement on heavenly authority, and therefore,

[19] Cf. the preliminary observations in the *Festschrift für F. Smend*, 1963, pp. 30ff.

[20] This is the view, for example, of W. Schmithals: 'Paulus und der historische Jesus', *ZNW* 53, 1962, pp. 145-60, especially p. 98; and Marxsen in the unpublished manuscript mentioned above.

as far as the resurrection of Jesus was concerned, certainly required no further factual elaboration. But secondly, the course of a narrative which aimed at coherence demanded that it should conclude with an event associated with the resurrection which took place where the passion did, in Jerusalem. But at the earliest period only the story of the women existed; from the point of view of their history as a distinctive form, the Galilean appearances had a quite different function in the tradition (i.e. that of authenticating particular leaders of the congregation), and were of no use at all here.

I imply by this: (1) That there was a story by the women about their discovery of the empty tomb, which was known at the time the primitive community was constituted in Jerusalem. In the course of the elaboration of the tradition of the passion it became the narrative framework of the preaching of the resurrection, in that the 'meaning' of the discovery by the women of the empty tomb—as the earthly evidence that Jesus' resurrection had taken place—was stylized in the form of the proclamation by the angel. (2) Apart from this story by the women, there were at this period no *narratives* of appearances of the risen Jesus which had been given any form in which they could be part of a tradition. I believe this is shown by the fact that in the whole New Testament we have only statements, but no elaborated narrative, of the oldest appearance, which is fundamental in the history of the Church, that to Peter. In addition to Mark 16.7, Luke 24.34 should be mentioned in this context. The story in John 21.1ff. is very late in the history of the tradition; moreover, on analysis it shows that the narrative elements of the complex of tradition which concerns the calling of the disciples were 'fugitive', and that here again it is the account of I Cor. 15.5 and Mark 16.7 which underlies them.

Thus we come to the end of the analytical parts of our study, and must now proceed to a synthesis. There is only room to set our view out in a number of brief theses:

1. It was the appearances of the risen Jesus in Galilee which inspired belief in the resurrection and led to the founding of the primitive community. On this basis, the resurrection of Jesus came to be a fundamental assumption in everything the community thought and did. Moving to Jerusalem, the community found in existence the women's story of the discovery of the

empty tomb. They regarded it as a confirmation of the belief in the resurrection which they had already brought with them from Galilee and—as something which had taken place at the site of the passion—it became so important that it was put into the form of a final pericope in the passion narrative. This was the only place in the living tradition of the primitive community in which the resurrection of Jesus formed the *theme* in a narrative context. Apart from this, it was used merely as the starting point of authentication formulae, which stated the authority of particular witnesses of the risen Jesus. There is, to say the least, no evidence that the resurrection formed a central theme of the Judaeo-Christian mission, while Luke 10 and Matt. 10 are evidence that the central theme of the mission of the disciples was Jesus' preaching of the kingdom of God.

2. At an early period diaspora Jews who were in Jerusalem came to believe in Jesus through contact with the primitive community. For them, the resurrection of Jesus was central and remained so. None of them had been disciples of Jesus. Moreover, whatever the reason may have been, they do not seem to have come into any closer contact with the primitive community of the disciples of Jesus. Thus they never came to be acquainted with the portrait of Jesus which the doctrinal tradition of the primitive community was alone able to provide, or at least did not place it at the centre of their tradition of belief. What they knew was the story of the passion and the resurrection, and the nucleus of their preaching was a brief summary of this: Jesus died and was raised by God; now he is with God in heaven and is the principal mediator of salvation in the final phase of time which is to come. When these Judaeo-Hellenistic Christians were driven out of Jerusalem, in every place in which, with extraordinary vigour, they founded Christian mission-communities, they exalted this *kerygma*, and it alone, into the central article of Christian belief, and from this nucleus gradually constructed a whole 'theology'. Under the powerful influence of the conceptual traditions of the Jewish diaspora and Hellenism there arose a cosmic christology here, which included in its assertions scarcely a word about the ministry and teaching of the historical Jesus himself. They were reduced to the two themes of the death and resurrection of Christ.

3. In the meantime a gradual Hellenization had been taking place in the realm of the original Jewish and Palestinian home of

the tradition concerning Jesus. It is under this influence that the earliest *stories* of appearances came into being, or alternatively, received the form which is familiar to us. The Hellenistic pattern of this tradition of the appearances can be seen in the Emmaus story (excluding the doctrinal discussion on the road) or in the story of the appearance to Mary Magdalene (John 20.14ff.). One can scarcely overestimate the Hellenistic trend, both here and in the mission sphere: here the ground was being prepared for the numerous varieties of gnosticism in early Christianity. But a powerful tendency which saw a grave danger in this withering away of the person of Jesus continued to dominate the tradition (or finally came to dominate it). It is this reverse tendency which explains the form given even to later resurrection stories, the classical example of which is the pre-Lucan story, Luke 24.36ff. Here the identity of the risen Christ with the pre-resurrection Jesus is demonstrated by means of the indubitable corporeality of his appearance: in his appearance he eats a piece of broiled fish before the eyes of the doubting disciples, who for a while cannot believe what they have seen, and so proves that he is not a spirit—as, in the view of the person who transmitted this tradition, some of the current resurrection stories represented him to be. This element of the tradition is misunderstood if one fails to appreciate this reaction, which seemed necessary from within a very special situation in the history of the tradition. This reaction played an important part in ensuring that the risen Christ remained identified with Jesus of Nazareth in common Christian tradition.

This concludes our survey of the history of the tradition of the primitive Christian testimony to the resurrection. At the beginning we emphasized that all questions concerning the way our present thought can deal with this primitive Christian tradition have been deliberately excluded. I am not as certain about this matter as Marxsen. I agree with him—and stress this once again—that it is impossible, and should not be required, that the primitive Christian tradition—in whatever way, with whatever theological artifice or with the aid of whatever hermeneutic theory—should be taken over without interpretation. Rather the question of an interpretation of the testimony to the resurrection which we can find convincing extends to the whole field. But it does not immediately imply the view that we should *always* have nothing to do with the assertions, concepts and tendencies of the past *as such*. What is necessary from an exegetical point of view is a more profound realization of the fact that the difficult task, for example, of mediating to the present day the tradition of contemporary Judaism, which is so closely interwoven with primitive Christian tradition, is not in itself hopeless. If it were nevertheless impossible in fact for us to mediate that tradition to our own time, that would mean admitting that primitive Christianity—at least that which was formed by Judaism—was no longer accessible to us *as a whole*, that is, including its meaning and purpose. One must take seriously the fact that it is impossible to have either the primitive Christian gospel, or even the God of primitive Christianity himself, apart from the history in which they were at work. To isolate the 'true' content of our Christian faith from its 'past' historical form also means to abandon *Jesus* as the central object of our faith. So long and so far as our present-day faith is essentially concerned to believe in God with respect to Jesus, it must also be concerned—for Jesus' sake—to interpret his whole history, including the earliest history of the Church with its position in the history of religion. How this can or ought to take place at the present day must be our immediate concern, once we have acknowledged that an attempt in this direction is necessary.

III

Gerhard Delling

THE SIGNIFICANCE OF THE RESURRECTION
OF JESUS FOR FAITH IN JESUS CHRIST

AN EXEGETICAL CONTRIBUTION

THE theme given to us[1] is not 'the resurrection of Jesus'. Instead, we have been specifically posed the question of the importance— according to the New Testament—of the resurrection of Jesus for faith in Jesus Christ. This means on the one hand, for example, that we are not expected to discuss in detail the resurrection narratives[2] and the numerous problems associated with them.[3] On the other hand, according to our terms of reference, we have to discuss the resurrection of Jesus in a much wider framework: we are concerned with whether faith in Christ is related to the resurrection of Jesus as a saving event at all. For of course we assume that the questions contained in our terms of reference refer to Jesus Christ as one in whom salvation is given, and in whom God acts to save; this is the reason for faith in Jesus Christ.

We have already hinted at the fact that of all the texts, I Cor. 15 has a very particular part to play in the treatment of our theme; this is true not only of the much discussed introductory passage vv. 1-11, but also of the section vv. 12-22, which is of particular importance for Paul in

---

[1] The literature that follows is referred to in the notes that follow only by the names of the authors, or by abbreviated titles: Hans Grass, *Ostergeschehen und Osterberichte*, 2nd ed. (1961); Wolfhart Pannenberg, *Grundzüge der Christologie* (1964); K. H. Rengstorf, *Die Auferstehung Jesu*, 4th ed. (1960); U. Wilckens, 'Das Offenbarungsverständnis in der Geschichte des Urchristentums', in W. Pannenberg (ed.), *Offenbarung als Geschichte*, 2nd ed. (1963), pp. 42-90; U. Wilckens, 'Der Ursprung der Überlieferung der Erscheinungen der Auferstandenen' in W. Joest/W. Pannenberg (eds.), *Dogma und Denkstrukturen* (1963), pp. 56-95.

[2] Cf. the limitation of his theme by Rengstorf, pp. 16f., cf. *op. cit.* p. 74, n. 1. Our theme touches that of E. Fascher, 'Die Auferstehung Jesu und ihr Verhältnis zur urchristlichen Verkündigung', *ZNW* 26, 1927, pp. 1-26.

[3] See the recent detailed study in Grass, pp. 15-53. His extensive bibliography in the 2nd ed. (pp. 329-34) is also relevant to our theme.

the framework of I Corinthians. There is good reason why Paul's statements have a somewhat dominant position in our discussion, for he provides the fullest material on the subject.[4] But otherwise we shall do what we can to make use of the whole New Testament in answering questions posed to us.

I

The earliest text in the New Testament to speak of the resurrection of Jesus from the point of view of the witnesses of it is I Cor. 15.4ff. Paul is quoting here,[5] as can be seen among other things from the presence of the expression, unusual in Paul, ὑπὲρ τῶν ἁμαρτιῶν ἡμῶν in v. 3[6] (cf. Gal. 1.4; the use of technical terms of rabbinic tradition should also be noted, I Cor. 15.3a). Thus Paul is repeating at least in part, right down to the form of words which he uses, what was handed on by him to the Corinthians in AD 50, which he had received sometime in the fourth decade of the century—and in all probability during the first half of that decade[7] (v. 11 explicitly mentions that this traditional

---

[4] We have moreover in the theologian Paul the only witness to the appearances who speaks directly to us (Grass, p. 259; Pannenberg, *Christologie*, p. 72).

[5] If he is assumed to have combined several passages; according to Wilckens (Ursprung, pp. 63-81, cf. the summary, pp. 80f.), there are six; Pannenberg, *Christologie*, p. 87, comments on this view without taking a line of his own.

[6] Cf. J. Jeremias: *Die Abendmahlsworte Jesu*, 3rd ed. (1960), p. 96; tr. *The Eucharistic Words of Jesus* (1966), p. 101. Of the other passages in Paul where this expression occurs in the plural (cf. *ibid.*) in Gal. 1.4 the continuing effect of the pre-Pauline prepositional expression is evident (cf. G. Delling: 'Partizipiale Gottesprädikationen in den Briefen des Neuen Testamentes', *ST* 17 [1963], pp. 1-59, esp. p. 37); in Col. 1.14 another pre-Pauline expression is taken up. In Rom. 7.5 ἁμαρτίαι is apparently used because Paul is not thinking merely of 'transgressions' (as elsewhere) but of the sinful desire which possesses power over man (Paul understands ἁμαρτία as a power). On I Cor. 15.17 cf. p. 84 below.

[7] Pannenberg, *Christologie*, p. 87; Grass, p. 95: 'Probably . . . soon after his conversion'; Wilckens, *Ursprung*, p. 62, n. 12, however, suggests Damascus. H. Conzelmann, 'Zur Analyse der Bekenntnisformel I Kor. 15.3-5', *Ev Th* 25 (1965), pp. 1-11, has recently attempted to refute the widely accepted demonstration of the Semitic origin of the passage by Jeremias (cf. n. 6 above), pp. 95-97 (ET, 101-3); cf. also Rengstorf, pp. 128f. For what is to my mind a remarkable assertion that 'the expression κατὰ τὰς γραφάς has no Semitic equivalent' (p. 6), Conzelmann appeals to Rengstorf, p. 51, n. 29, who, however, expresses himself much more cautiously: 'An *exact* verbal parallel in *rabbinic* late Judaism to κατὰ τὰς γραφάς *has not yet* been shown' (italics mine). To ı))ı with the accusative, in the sense of 'according to', the Hebrew *l°pi* provides a likely parallel; cf. for example 1 QS 3.23, 'in accordance with the

formula agrees with the whole apostolic tradition, that is, that of Jerusalem in particular). Thus it takes us back to a very early stage of primitive Christian tradition. The nature of this tradition shows that its origins lie in the very days in which the disciples became certain of the resurrection of Jesus.

Paul, of course (and the same is true of the resurrection narratives, which are later from the literary point of view, and of the New Testament as a whole), does not speak of the disciples becoming certain, but of the ὀφθῆναι[8] of Christ (in the whole section I Cor. 15.1-22 Paul invariably uses the title Χριστός, which in all his writings refers particularly to the crucified and risen Jesus). The first ὤφθη (we must say something more about the expression itself later) occurs in I Cor. 15 (v. 5), and is inextricably bound up with other statements in this fragment of primitive Christian tradition. The passage consists of vv. 3b-5a at least.

In it, the attention is drawn at a first glance to two parallel sentences of several phrases, both beginning with a verb and concluding with the phrase 'according to the scriptures'; but the intervening phrases are not parallel in content. The first, 'for our sins' clearly represents an interpretation of the preceding verb (the death of Christ takes away the guilt of men); by contrast, 'on the third day' in the first instance gives a purely temporal qualification of the statement concerning the resurrection. But it is obvious that the two central phrases are each closely associated with the verb, and that the expression 'according to the scriptures' refers in each case to the whole of what proceeds it; this is immediately obvious in the case of the first sentence. In this case, it is wholly probable, in view of the preceding words ὑπὲρ τῶν ἁμαρτιῶν ἡμῶν, that 'according to the scriptures' includes a reference to Isa. 53.12 (Paul may also be referring to this passage elsewhere, cf. Rom. 4.25a); the use of the plural, however, implies that the Old Testament as a whole bears witness to the saving significance of the death of Jesus; conformity with the

---

mysteries of God'. The expression does not occur elsewhere in the New Testament in the plural, but is found in the singular in James 2.8; it also occurs six times in the Septuagint (for *kikᵉtab* II Chron. 35.4; Ezra 6.17). Conzelmann, however, at least does not deny completely that the formula may have its origin in Jerusalem (p. 8).

[8] The same verb is used in the active in Mark 16.7; Matt. 28.7, 10; John 20.18, 25, 29; cf. Matt. 28.17; Luke 24.39; John 20.20, 27.

scriptures as such is of decisive importance for primitive Christianity, for this was the source of its certainty that the death of Jesus was rooted in God's purpose of salvation. It seems right to understand the second 'according to the scriptures', referring to the resurrection of Christ on the third day, in a similar comprehensive sense. Examples of the use of specific scriptural testimonies to the resurrection of Jesus can be found in Acts 2.24-28, and 13.34-37, where use is made of Ps. 16.8-11 and Isa. 55.3 in association with Ps. 16.10.[9] It has been supposed that Hos. 6.2 is the specific text applied to the resurrection on the third day; this suggestion has been repeated in recent works.[10] But what we have said does not mean that in I Cor. 15.4 the scriptural testimony to the resurrection on the third day is given prominence; the term 'on the third day' is evidently associated from the first with the announcement of the fact of the resurrection. The discovery of the empty tomb (and according to Luke 24.1, 13ff. and John 20.19, also the first appearance to the eleven) is firmly associated with the third day according to the synoptic tradition, and this is the basis of the catechetical statement 'raised on the third day'.

But the two sentences which immediately strike the attention in I Cor. 15.3f. are linked not merely by the phrase 'according to the scriptures', but also by the intervening and syntactically independent clause ἐτάφη. In fact the catechetical passage I Cor. 15.3-5 is composed of four affirmative clauses co-ordinated by the conjunction ὅτι (which does not mean, as has recently been supposed, that Paul here brings together four statements which were originally separate;[11] the three ὅτι in vv. 4f. serve at the same time

---

[9] Justin, *Dial. c. Tryph.* 16.5; 97.2; 118.1, sees the resurrection of Jesus as prophesied in Isa. 57.2. By a different punctuation of the phrases of the Septuagint text, which is probably already assumed in *Dial.* 16.5 (*Apol.* 48.6 takes it in a different sense), Justin obtains the form of the text in *Dial.* 97.2; 118.1: ἡ ταφὴ αὐτοῦ ἦρται ἐκ τοῦ μέσου. In 97.2 reference is also made to Isa. 53.9.

[10] *TWNT* II, p. 952; cf. Grass, pp. 136-8; U. Wilkens, *Die Missionsreden der Apostelgeschichte* (1961), p. 78, n. 4; p. 143, n. 2; J. Dupont, 'Ressuscité "le troisième jour" ', *Biblica*, 40 (1959), pp. 742-61, esp. pp. 756-61, etc.

[11] Wilckens, *Ursprung*, p. 73. What is the meaning of the sentence: ὅτι *recitativum* 'always *introduces* in the New Testament kerygmatic or homological formulae' (Wilkens' italics?) In Paul himself ὅτι *recitativum* comes before quotations from the Old Testament (Rom. 4.17; 8.36; 9.17; I Cor. 14.21; II Cor. 6.16; Gal. 3.8, 10), as well as in other contexts which have nothing to do with *kerygma*, homology and the like; cf. Rom. 3.8; Gal. 1.23; I Cor. 14.25; II Thess. 3.10). Wilckens is presumably thinking of passages

to separate and emphasize each one of the four statements which are co-ordinated with one another.[12] Ἐτάφη links the content of ἀπέθανεν and ἐγήγερται. The dead Jesus was actually buried— here 'he was buried' confirms 'he died'; in the ancient world interment sealed and confirmed death.[13] And it was the Jesus who was buried, who was also raised. The part played by the phrase ἐτάφη demonstrates the personal identity of the crucified and the risen Jesus, and therefore at the same time shows how God's saving action is fully comprehended in Christ, as can also be seen from other statements in the New Testament.

According to Wilckens, the statements concerning the appearances of the risen Jesus which are preserved in I Cor. 15.5, 7 were originally 'authentication formulae on which special authority was based' (*Ursprung*, p. 75); the 'appearance to "all the apostles" ' is concerned with the 'sacral and juridical constituting of the apostolate' (p. 69), etc. The only evidence for the thesis that primitive Christianity did not speak of the appearance of the risen Jesus in the form of a narrative, but only in order to authenticate a particular authority, is to be found in the statements of Paul, in particular in Gal. 1.15f. and I Cor. 9.1. These Pauline statements, however, are far from providing sufficient grounds for the view that the statements concerning the appearances to the twelve, etc., were intended in the first instance to authenticate their authority. (This does not mean that we are denying that appearances to particular persons have a decisive influence upon their status in primitive Christianity.)

Wilckens' thesis is obviously connected with a specific view of a history of tradition (cf. *Ursprung*, p. 86, n. 72). According to this, neither Paul, the 'missionary tradition of the Syrian Church from

---

such as I Cor. 11.23; Phil. 2.11. But we must point to the difference in the handling of the beginning of related series of statements with the aid of realtive clauses: this is sometimes done by means of a single relative (cf. Phil. 2.6), and sometimes by several, so articulating the statements together (1 Peter 2.22, 23, 24). See also the following note.

[12] In *Ursprung*, p. 74 Wilckens supposes it possible (as a first alternative) that the 'mention of the burial of Jesus in the early missionary tradition (I Cor. 15.4a)' involves the use of 'a formula "died and was buried" which forms a single whole'. But in such a formula ὅτι would always have been absent before ἐτάφη, and this means that Paul would have been responsible for introducing it in the epistle (cf. note 11 above).

[13] Cf. Acts 2.29 (see 13.36; '[he] saw corruption'). Certainly what has been said above is not clear in every passage: the burial can also be adduced as a proof of the (last) necessary service to the dead body. But even where its mention simply seems to complete the account of the death of someone, it at the same time confirms his death.

which Paul went out' (*Offenbarung*, p. 71, n. 55), nor the Hellenists in Jerusalem possessed any narrative tradition about Jesus. This view is based solely upon the silence of the New Testament epistles. Wilckens is obviously bound to suppose that in Jerusalem (Gal. 1.18; 2.1ff.) Paul did not come into contact with any fixed pre-synoptic tradition concerning Jesus, or at least that it did not interest him, and that either Peter—even supposing one does not accept the statement of Acts that Barnabas moved from Jerusalem to Antioch (Acts .11.22-26)—must have said nothing in Antioch about Jesus' ministry in Galilee, or else the Antiochenes must have taken no notice of what he said (Gal. 2.11ff.).

Although the view of the history of the tradition taken by Wilckens is not convincing, what is possible is that the main task of the tradition of the appearances was from the first the authentication of the preaching of the risen Jesus. The formulae in I Cor. 15.5, 7 are obviously catechetical in their nature, and do not exclude the possible existence of a narrative of the appearance of the risen Jesus to the 'twelve'—in an earlier form of the narratives we possess (cf. Rengstorf, p. 85)—however unlikely it is that there were accounts of all the appearances which are named in I Corinthians.

The fourth affirmative clause introduced by ὅτι in I Cor. 15.3-5 clearly provides Paul with the testimony of the witnesses to the statements 'he was raised on the third day', which is indispensable to him in the context of I Cor. 15. It is wholly impossible to accept that ὤφθη originally formed the conclusion of the catechetical passage, and that therefore no witness was named at all (as has sometimes been suggested recently[14]); it is certainly not possible to base such a view on the suggestion of a complete parallel between ἐτάφη and ὤφθη. The word ἐτάφη by itself, and by its position between the sentences which here precede and follow it, does what it is supposed to do; the word ὤφθη requires that the person to whom the appearance was given should be mentioned (this is found even with ὀπτανόμενος in Acts 1.3, which refers to something which took place repeatedly; ὤφθη in each case refers only a single manifestation).

On the other hand, it is conceivable that the received catechetical passage once concluded with v. 5b (the clauses in vv. 6f.) are no longer linked by ὅτι to παρέδωκα or παρέλαβον.[15] This

---

[14] E. Bammel, 'Herkunft und Funktion der Traditionselemente in I Kor. 15.1-11', *TZ* 11 (1955), pp. 401-19, esp. pp. 402f. The opposite view is put by F. Hahn, *Christologische Hoheitstitel* (1963), pp. 198f: On I Cor. 15.3ff. cf. pp. 197-211.

[15] ἔπειτα in Paul can introduce further members of a series within a list,

would mean that for the sake of a comprehensive demonstration of the testimony to the resurrection, a demonstration which he based on the ὤφθη, Paul added to the list of witnesses in the received passage from other traditions. He is obviously concerned to name as many witnesses as possible, and similarly to give as full a list as possible of the appearances[16]; it is moreover not without importance, according to v. 6, that it is still possible to question some of the witnesses.[17] Finally, the group of persons formed by the eye-witnesses of the resurrection apparently have a part to play in I Cor. 15; the word 'they' in v. 11 seems to refer to those of the witnesses of the resurrection who in some pre-eminent way proclaim it. There were none of the 'twelve' and there was no apostle who did not in the same way proclaim the resurrection of Jesus as a witness of the ὤφθη.

The word ὀφθῆναι[18] (which also occurs in other contexts in the New Testament) has a distinctive semantic history, especially

without any temporal sense: cf. I Cor. 12.28. But this does not prevent ἔπειτα and εἶτα in I Cor. 15.6f. from being temporal in meaning, as is most probably the case with εἶτα in v. 5 (cf. ἐσχατον πάντων v. 8). But it should be considered whether the appearances mentioned in vv. 6f. may not have taken place some time after the first two.

[16] In Acts 1.3 'many proofs' are mentioned (the expression is interpreted by the imperfect particle which follows); in Luke 24 three are mentioned (vv. 13ff., 34, 36ff.). The expression used in Acts 1.3 does not necessarily mean that the author was able to list other appearances or to describe them; it may be a generalized statement about the forty days.

[17] Cf. for example Wilckens, *Ursprung*, p. 63, n. 13. I cannot understand the explanation in H. W. Bartsch, 'Die Argumentation des Paulus in I Kor. 15.3-11', *ZNW* 55 (1964), pp. 262-74, that in v. 6 Paul is carrying out 'a *reductio ad absurdum* of the thesis of the Corinthians . . ., that immortality is obtained by faith in the appearances of Christ': 'Even some of the witnesses of the resurrection have fallen asleep! How can you Corinthians believe that there is no longer a resurrection of the dead, because death has already been overcome' (p. 273). Is the death of the witnesses of an appearance of the risen Jesus to be regarded as different from that of other Christians in this context (I Cor. 11.30)?

[18] In order to interpret the way in which the experience of the resurrection appearances as such is conceived, Wilckens refers to Jewish apocalyptic. But the possibility of a comparison is limited on both sides, as Wilckens himself finally admits (*Ursprung*, pp. 85-90). 'In the light of comparative religion' (p. 88), the manner in which they are conceived in the New Testament remains entirely a part of the Jewish background; Wilckens himself, however, makes clear (pp. 85f.) that for Paul the appearances of the risen Jesus are clearly distinguished from other revelations that are received (cf. II Cor. 12.1ff.). As far as their content is concerned, the framework of Jewish conceptions is shattered not merely by the specific event of the raising of Jesus, but also by the particular significance which is accorded to it.

in the Septuagint, although the special significance of the word in the statements concerning the appearances of the risen Jesus cannot be derived directly from this. It has been shown that in the Septuagint ὀφθῆναι can signify the coming of God to someone without God being visible.[19] But it is always clear in the case of the resurrection appearances, that ὀφθῆναι does not merely mean to reveal oneself as present,[20] but to be manifested as visibly present.[21] With respect to the ὤφθη of the risen Jesus which had occurred to him, Paul says 'I have seen the Lord' (I Cor. 9.1); in the narratives of the empty tomb the promise is made to the disciples that in Galilee they would see the risen Jesus (Mark 16.7; Matt. 28.7, 10); in John 20.18, 25 the witnesses state 'I (or we) have seen the Lord' (cf. also Luke 24.16, 31). In the statements concerning the visible appearances of the risen Jesus ὤφθη is certainly always related to a person ('to Cephas', 'to me', etc.; cf. ἀποκαλύψαι ... ἐν ἐμοί (Gal. 1.16); this ἐν moreover, is not the spatial 'in', but likewise signifies the person towards whom the act of God is carried out;[22] cf. also ἐφανερώθη τοῖς μαθηταῖς (John 21.14). But that according to the New Testament understanding this seeing is real is shown by the fact that the risen Jesus appears in bodily form, and that the personal identity of the earthly and the risen Jesus is affirmed.

When Paul speaks in I Cor. 9.1 of seeing the 'Lord', there is no

[19] Cf. W. Michaelis, *TWNTV*, pp. 51, 330. Cf. the discussions in R. Rend, torff, 'Die Offenbarungsvorstellungen im Alten Israel', in Pannenberg-*Offenbarung*, pp. 21-41, esp. pp. 23-25, where more distinctions are made. Cf. with this and with what follows Hahn (see n. 14 above) pp. 206ff.—In fact according to the context ὀφθῆναι can signify a real seeing, as for example of the glory of God in the clouds in Ex. 16. 10; Lev. 9.6, 23, etc.

[20] W. Michaelis, *TWNT* V, p. 331 on Ex. 3.2, 4, 16. The assumptions which can be made for God's revealing of himself without becoming visible are not true of Jesus. The only mention of a vision of God in the New Testament is that in Rev. 4.1ff., and this does not take place upon earth.

[21] It cannot be argued with certainty that the passage includes the idea of being visibly made known by God (Rengstorff, p. 56: 'God showed visibly', and pp. 57, 58, with a reference to Acts 10.40). The statements in Acts concerning the ὀφθῆναι of Jesus can in themselves be so understood, cf. 10.40; whether the author understood the wording of 9.17; 13.3.; 26.16 in such a sense is uncertain from the other occasions on which he uses ὀφθῆναι., cf especially 7.2, also 2.3, etc., and also the use of ὀφθῆναι in other New Testament works.

[22] Cf. W. Bauer, *Griechisch-deutsches Wörterbuch zu den Schriften des Neuen Testaments*, 5th ed. (1958), s.v. ἐν, I 2 (where Bauer includes Gal. 1.16) and IV 4a. (ET, W. F. Arndt and F. W. Gingrich, *A Greek-English Lexicon of the New Testament and Other Early Christian Literature*, [1957].)

question that he understands this to mean seeing him in the form of a bodily resurrection (otherwise he could not base the certainty of the bodily resurrection on the ὤφθη, in the way he does in I Cor. 15.4ff.). In fact Paul obviously holds quite definite conceptions of the corporeality of the risen Jesus seen by him (and others).[23] The statements concerning the resurrection body in I Cor. 15.35-49 as a whole are evidently not said merely of the new bodies of Christians. For Paul sees the latter as corresponding entirely to the body of the risen Christ. This is also the case in the brief summary statement in Phil. 3.21:[24] he who is to come in the *parousia* will make the form of our 'lowly body' like that of his glorious body (this is the sense of the strongly emphasized statements which make a causal inference from the resurrection of Jesus to that of a Christian; cf. below). The short statement in Phil. 3 is confirmed, among other passages, by I Cor. 15.49: just as we have borne the image of man created from dust (earth), the image of Adam, so we will also bear the image of the heavenly man (the word 'image' does not weaken the correspondence, neither in the first, nor in the second instance). Paul is undoubtedly referring in the latter assertion to the body of the risen Christ, the 'second Adam' (v. 47). Christ is also the author of the new humanity (cf. also Rom. 5.12ff.) with regard to the mode of existence in the world to come (cf. v. 45). That is, Christ is risen 'in glory', 'in power' (v. 43). Paul makes a total distinction between the resurrection body and the earthly body (it is not 'flesh and blood' v. 50); he characterizes it by the word πνευματικός as belonging in its nature to God's new world (v. 41)[25]; and evidently understands it as newly created (v. 38); cf. the differentiation in v. 44b; I believe it is also possible to refer here to II Cor.

[23] On the following cf. also Rengstorf, pp. 80-86, Pannenberg, *Christologie*, pp. 71-73.

[24] On this passage cf. J. Schneider, *TWNT* VII, p. 958; W. Grundmann, *ibid.*, p. 788, *ibid.*, VIII, p. 22.

[25] The Pauline view of the peculiar nature of the resurrection body cannot in my view be derived from the conceptions of Jewish apocalyptic, in the way in which this is done in Pannenberg's *Christologie*. For Pannenberg the main reference is clearly provided by Syr. Bar. (50f.), that is, a work from the end of the first century AD. If 'the question . . . of the nature of the transformation . . . as a whole . . . first became acute in the first century AD' in Judaism (p. 76), one may at least ask whether Paul, or Jesus (Mark 12.25 and parallels), or at least primitive Christianity, did not play a decisive part in the development of such conceptions. At least I would hold the view that a different emphasis should be sought, cf. also the following notes.

5.1.[26] But at the same time he regards both the mortal and incorruptible bodies (v. 42) together, from the point of view of the personal unity of man (I Cor. 6.13f.).

We must not overlook the fact that the statements of the resurrection narrative which we possess in a later form are analogous to those in Paul at least insofar as they make clear that the body of the risen Jesus is different in nature from that of the earthly Jesus (Luke 24.31, 36; John 20.14, 19; on the other hand, they emphasize the correspondence between the one and the other: Luke 24.39a; John 20.20, 27). This is done, of course, in a different way from that of Paul, in concrete narrative terms; certain versions of the narratives, which give a crude emphasis to the correspondence between the body of the earthly Jesus and that of the risen Jesus, would certainly not have been acceptable to Paul (especially the statements about the risen Jesus etc., cf. Luke 24.39b, 41-43). But the fundamental agreements must not be overlooked; and they cannot be dismissed as Hellenistic.[27]

In spite of the limited circle of witnesses to the appearances, the revelation of the resurrection which took place is of universally valid significance. Paul makes a decisive appeal to the eye witnesses of the risen Jesus in the framework of his whole preaching; the resurrection narratives of the gospel were written (and, in some form or other, had been previously handed down) for the same purpose. In the missionary speeches of Acts, special reference is constantly made to the twelve as witnesses of the risen Jesus (2.32; 3.15; 4.33; 10.41; 13.31, cf. 5.32; cf. 1.22).[28] The statements of the witnesses of the resurrection became fundamental to the faith of Christians: οὕτως κηρύσσομεν καὶ οὕτως ἐπιστεύσατε (I Cor. 15.11).

Paul clearly understands the repeated ὤφθη as a confirmation of ἐγήγερται found in the perfect here and in I Cor. 15.4, 12, 13, 16,

[26] Pannenberg's discussions (cf. note 25 above) proceed in the case of Judaism mainly from the concept of transformation, which seems to correspond to the Pauline ἀλλάσσεσθαι (I Cor. 15.51f.). Paul uses ἀλλάσσεσθαι here instead of ἐγείρεσθαι because it is also applicable to those who are still alive. That in their case, by contrast to those who have fallen asleep, he is not thinking of the provision of another body, is unlikely in the view of the purpose of the passage (cf. A. Schlatter, Paulus, der Bote Jesus [1934], p. 444). In the events of the end the νεκροί and ἡμεῖς are equated. Paul also speaks of ἐγείρεσθαι in the form of a passive personal statement.

[27] Cf. e.g. E. Schweizer, TWNT VI, pp. 419, lines 1ff.

[28] Even assuming that the missionary sermons are much later than Paul.

17, 20; II Tim. 2.8; [Mark] 16.14; the question in I Cor. 15.12ff. is that of the resurrection of the dead; Paul defends it on the basis of the raising of Jesus, which vv. 1-11 show to have been witnessed.[29] Those who witnessed the risen Jesus confirmed the fact that he had been raised; the New Testament does not tell of any witnesses of the process of the resurrection itself (not even in Matthew; the guards are frightened by the *angel*, 28.4). Paul emphasizes that the raising itself is an act of God (I Cor. 15.15, etc., cf. below); moreover, the ἠγέρθη of the synoptics must be taken in the same sense (Mark 16.6; Matt. 28.6f.; Luke 24.34; John 2.22 cf. ζωοποιηθείς, I Peter 3.18). The New Testament confirms this in numerous sentences active in form (nowadays these are no longer explained as 'Deutero-Pauline writing' without qualification): Heb. 13.20; I Peter 1.21; Acts 3.15; 4.10; 5.30; 10.40; 13.30, 37, etc. (further references to Paul's epistles are given below).

We should not forget that the statement 'who . . . raised', with God as the subject, frequently occurs in the New Testament epistles in the form of a participle clause. The participle clause is a form much used for set expressions. In Rom. 4.24 Christians are described as those who believe 'in him that raised (participle) from the dead Jesus our Lord'. Christians confess[30] the God who raised Jesus from the dead; here God is characterized by his main decisive action.[31] This is evidently a deliberate alteration of a divine title in the form of a participle, used in Judaism: 'Who makes living the dead', the end of the second benediction of the *shemoneh 'esrah* (Paul takes it up in Rom. 4.17, cf. II Cor. 1.9). Primitive Christianity made the distinction between itself and

[29] Cf. H. Braun: 'Exegetische Rundglossen zum 1 Korintherbrief' *Gesammelte Studien zum Neuen Testament und seiner Umwelt* (1962), pp. 178-204; he says that in I Cor. 15.1-11 the raising of Jesus is regarded as an historically demonstrable fact (p. 200, following Bultmann). In order to free Paul from Bultmann's charge that he is using a fatal line of argument here (Bartsch, pp. 261f.), Bartsch (cf. n. 17) attempts to show that in I Cor. 15.3-11 Paul is concerned to show that the resurrection of Jesus is essentially linked with the cross. 'Thus here too the emphasis is wholly on the Pauline preaching of the Crucified' (p. 271). For Paul, the line of argument which Bultmann rightly understands (although he wrongly condemns it) in I Cor. 15.3ff. is obviously in no sense fatal.

[30] By contrast to the 'fools', Polycarp, *Phil.* 2.1, where I Peter 1.21 is quoted, but altered.

[31] For the particle statements concerning 'him who . . . raised' cf. Delling (cf. n. 6 above), pp. 31-34.

Judaism, that it believed in him who raised Jesus from the dead. Whereas the Jewish divine title refers to the future act of God, the Christian title signifies that the eschatological action of God has already begun—in Jesus Christ. 'Ο ἐγείρας occurs as an independent divine title notably in Gal. 1.1 in a context where at first sight there is no apparent reason for it. This is, however, a set form, the introductory greeting in which other similar statements are given special weight elsewhere—Paul's apostolate derives from the raising of Jesus Christ from the dead (further expressions with the same participle clause in Rom. 4.24; 8.11a.b.; II Cor. 4.14; Col. 2.12. The clause is given a particularly full form in Heb. 13.20); here the participle which is the divine title: 'who brought again from the dead', is likewise not imposed by the context, but in form is extremely solemn.

II

It has become more or less obvious that the resurrection of Jesus and the carefully specified testimony to it is important for the faith of primitive Christianity. In what precise sense is this true? We shall not begin again with the Pauline epistles, but with Acts. Here the raising of Jesus is mentioned twelve times, and in a way which lays great stress upon it. Acts 17 shows that according to the author the gospel of the resurrection of Jesus had a decisive part to play even in preaching to the Gentiles, in spite of the rejection it encountered (vv. 18, 32): this is summed up in the statement that even before the philosophers of Athens Paul preached 'Jesus and the resurrection' (v. 18), and the sermon on the Aeropagus, which goes to such lengths to find a point of contact, concludes with a statement concerning the man whom God manifested as destined to be the future judge of the world by raising him from the dead (v. 31; cf. 10.42). Thus the author of Acts is not merely making a tactical move, when in Acts 23.6 (and 24.15, 31 should be understood in a similar sense) he makes Paul claim that he was being accused as one who held a belief in the resurrection, which—this is the natural implication—he preached of Jesus (cf. 25.19). According to 4.2 Peter and John were in fact arrested precisely for proclaiming the resurrection of the dead in the Lord Jesus, and in the account given of the primitive Jerusalem community, the resurrection of Jesus is mentioned on its own as the content of the 'testimony' (4.33).

Of course a special link is frequently made between the death and the resurrection of Jesus. This takes place in Jerusalem in the parallel between 'you killed—God raised' (2.23f.; 3.15; 4.10; 5.30), and elsewhere, in front of Jews and 'those who feared God', on the pattern 'the people of Jerusalem brought him to death—God raised him' (13.27-30; 10.39). The death and raising of Jesus are also linked in statements concerning the scriptural proofs that were used in the synagogues of the diaspora, 17.3; 26.22f. (cf. Luke 24.26; and I Cor. 15.3f.). But even although it is sometimes possible for a scriptural proof to be mentioned as it were with special reference to the suffering of Jesus (3.18), and even though there is one statement that the killing of Jesus took place according to the fixed will and purpose of God (2.23), the author of Acts never says anything about the reason for the παθεῖν (although he may be close to this in 10.43).[32] This is all the more striking, since—even in the sermon on the Areopagus (17.30)—he quite clearly lays repeated stress upon the universal necessity of repentance (2.38; 3.19; 5.31; 11.18; 20.21; 26.20), and puts forward the promise of the forgiveness of sins, which is wholly associated with Jesus (5.31; 10.43; 13.38; 26.18).

But the forgiveness of sins, as all the prophets testify (10.43), is given in him whom God has exalted to be judge at his right hand (5.31, cf. 13.37f.; cf. also 2.36). It is in accordance with this that in the sermons a special point is made of setting out the scriptural proofs of the promise of the raising of Jesus by God (2.24ff.; 13.34ff.; cf. above). According to Acts, the significance of the raising of Jesus lies in the fact that Jesus is thereby confirmed or constituted as him on whose name—that is, on whose person— the possibility of repentance, forgiveness and therefore redemption at the judgment depends.

Since what is said about the resurrection in Acts is uttered in the context of missionary preaching, it occurs in the form of indicative clauses which proclaim or impart it (the participle form assumes knowledge of the event, when it characterizes God as him who raised Jesus; it summed up the community's confession of faith). It is presented in expressions which are frequently either the same in wording, or correspond exactly: 3.15; 4.10; 13.30, 31; 10.40a; 5.30a; 17.31 (the participle which occurs here, and here alone, is from a stylistic point of view not what

---

[32] In Luke, however, Mark 10.45 and parallels are lacking.

we find in the epistles, but corresponds to the indicative we have mentioned); 2.24, 32 (in the last three passages ἀνιστάναι—transitive—is used,[33] but elsewhere ἐγείρω, only in fact in the form ἤγειρεν). It is also possible for Jesus to be spoken of explicitly as rising (ἀναστῆναι) 10.41; 17.3; ἀναστῆναι occurs in Acts in place of ἐγερθῆναι—the passive forms of ἐγείρω are not used of Jesus in Acts. The phrase ἐκ νεκρῶν belongs to the received form of words (3.15; 4.10; 13.30, 34; 17.31; cf. 10.41; 17.3; cf. 4.2).

In every form of expression in Acts the witnesses of the appearances of Jesus are referred to as witnesses of his raising: God had raised him, and of this (to this) we are witnesses: 2.32; 3.15; cf. 5.32. In more exact formal terms, it is also possible to say that God raised him on the third day and made him visible not to his 'people', but to the witnesses previously chosen by God, that is, to us, who ate and drank with him, after he had risen from the dead (10.40f.). In this somewhat fuller statement from Peter's sermon in the house of Cornelius, one can see that the author is just as capable as Paul of placing side by side the raising on the third day and the appearing before chosen witnesses. This does not imply the literary dependence of the sermon at Caesarea on I Cor. 15; rather, the similarity goes back to the common tradition, with regard to the substance of what is said. At the same time it is clear that the testimony to the resurrection by the twelve in Acts is important in the same way as Paul: whether it is 'Luke' or Paul, they proclaim the same risen Jesus (I Cor. 15.11).

The interpretation which sees Jesus as raised for the sake of his exaltation[34] and is found elsewhere in the New Testament, is also present in Acts 2.32f.; in 5.30a, 31 both are found together in the same way (the clause mentioning the raising is here given

---

[33] Whether ἀνιστάναι carries the meaning 'raised' in 13.33 is disputed; in 3.26 it is improbable, cf. ἀπέστειλεν—the aim of the sending of the earthly Jesus was already that of saving repentance. What we have gone on to say about ἀναστῆναι belongs in the context of the fact that ἀναστῆναι and ἐγερθῆναι are never distinguished in the New Testament (as is constantly asserted) by the latter referring to the resurrection as something which is carried out upon a person, while the former signifies an act he carries out himself. Mark 12.23, 25; Luke 16.31; I Thess. 4.16; John 11.23f.; Acts 9.40 certainly do not imply that the dead rise up themselves; cf. the Test. Jud. 25.1, 4; Test. B. 10.6f.; Ps. Sal. 3.12. On the other hand ἐγείρεσθαι—or ἐγερθῆναι—in themselves can have the general sense 'to lift oneself up', cf. on the LXX, A. Oepke *TWNT* II, pp. 333, 340ff.

[34] For references cf. n. 52 below.

emphatic pre-eminence over that concerning the crucifixion); the statement concerning his glorification in 3.13 points in the same direction (cf. v. 15). It can be confirmed that salvation in Acts is particularly dependent upon the (name of) the raised (and exalted) Jesus.

Thus in Acts the raising of Jesus is above all christologically significant: through being raised, Jesus becomes above all the one in whose name salvation is given; it is faith in the risen Jesus, as we saw, which brings the possibility of repenting and receiving forgiveness, and therefore brings salvation at the judgment (10.41-43). We do not learn in Acts how precisely this is based upon the resurrection of Jesus. This observation is probably related to the fact that no specific saving significance is given in Acts for the death of Jesus. One might say that the author simply puts forward the fact of the resurrection of Jesus, and of the significance of the 'name' of the risen Jesus for salvation.

In the Gospel of John (20.9), the resurrection of Jesus is also seen as deriving from God's plan of salvation; it comes under the divine δεῖ, which includes the idea of the pre-determined decree of God and the fulfilment of the scripture in one; God's plan of salvation can be made out from the scripture. The Gospel of John also emphasizes, cf. Luke 24.44-46, that his δεῖ was first understood by the disciples and perceived in the scripture after the resurrection had taken place (John 20.9 and similarly 2.22; the word of Jesus here refers to v. 19, which in v. 21 is interpreted on the basis of scripture; as in I Cor. 15.4 and John 20.9 no scripture reference is given). For the Gospel of John, the resurrection of Jesus is above all the prerequisite of his going to the Father; the two are not simply equated: 20.17 (where the word used is ἀναβαίνειν, cf. 6.22). The going to the Father takes place through the resurrection; thus this becomes a prerequisite for the sending of the Paraclete (16.7; cf. 7.39, and also 20.22) and for the activity of the exalted Christ as a whole. Great weight is placed on the meetings with the risen Christ immediately after the resurrection; it is these which bring about full knowledge of who Christ is, and full fellowship with Jesus (14.9f.; cf. 16.23a), and enduring joy (the way to which is necessarily provided by Good Friday; 16.16-22). What was received in the encounters with the risen Jesus is continued in the constant union of him who has gone to the Father with his followers (cf. 17.23; 14.13).

The activity of the exalted Christ is seen as beginning quite definitely with the post-resurrection encounters. As in Matthew (28.19) and Luke (24.47f.; cf. Acts 1.8) the risen Christ sends the disciples into the world (John 20.21 and 17.18; cf. the giving of the commission in 21.15-17). But as in the synoptic gospels, the immediate purpose of the resurrection narratives is that of a testimony to the resurrection. In John, this takes place once again not merely through the empty tomb (insofar as ἐπίστευσεν in 20.8 may be translated 'he was convinced'[35]), as such, but in the encounters with the risen Christ. Here his personal identity with the earthly Jesus (20.16) and with the Crucified One (20.20, 25, 27) is explicitly emphasized. In 20.29—blessed are those who believe (come to believe) without having seen—the Gospel of John is not opposed to I Cor. 15.5ff.; the testimony of those who encountered the risen Christ is the basis, in both, of the certainty of those who believe after them (John 20.29; I Cor. 15.11).

In the synoptics, the empty tomb becomes a proof of the resurrection only through the interpretation of the angel (Mark 16.1-8 and parallels). The tradition of the empty tomb clearly exists from the very first[36] alongside that of the appearances of the risen Christ. The decisive appearance is clearly seen to be that to the eleven (Luke 24.36-49; Matt. 28.16-20; cf. John 20.19-23; cf. also Mark 16.7). As implied above, it is associated with the missionary command of the risen Christ to the disciples (and this is so in every version in the gospels): the risen Christ acts upon the world through his disciples (in I Cor. 15.4ff. this theme is not visible,[37] though it is in Gal. 1.16). The whole authority to

[35] W. Nauck, 'Die Bedeutung des leeren Grabes für den Glauben an den Auferstandenen', *ZNW* 47 (1956), pp. 243-67, esp. p. 254.

[36] Hans Frh. v. Campenhausen, *Der Anlauf der Ostereignisse und das leere Grab*, Sitzungsberichte der Heidelberger Akad. Phil.-hist. Kl. 1952, IV, 2nd ed. (1958).

[37] It cannot be concluded from Gal. 1.15f.; I Cor. 9.1; 3, 5; (as Wilckens, *Ursprung* p. 67, supposes) that 'the formulae in I Cor. 15.5 and 7 . . . are authentication formulae for the special authority' of those who are named in them—from the very first (*ibid.*, p. 75). That I Cor. 15.9f. to some extent echoes the defence of Paul's apostolate (more precisely in v. 10; in v. 9 Paul accuses himself!) is only evident to someone who knows Galatians and I and II Corinthians; but there it is Paul's particular situation at the moment which is at issue. Pannenberg, *Christologie*, p. 91, emphasizes that by mentioning the appearance which he underwent in I Cor. 15 Paul 'is not thinking of his commissioning as an apostle, but of the testimony to the reality of the risen Christ'. Nor is there any suggestion of an authentication by the ὤφθη in v. 9f. Cf. pp. 81f. above.

exercise God's kingly rule is given to Jesus as the risen Christ; it is carried out above all in the mission 'to all nations' (Matt. 28.18; οὖν v. 19; the promise in v. 20 is made in the first instance of the messengers and their ministry).

The empty tomb and the appearances of the risen Christ show that he who was crucified (Mark 16.6 and parallels) is alive (Luke 24.25) and at work as the exalted Christ. That the raising of Jesus is the decisive event of God's saving act is hinted at in the synoptic gospels in the context of the prophecy of his suffering, which also makes the raising (or resurrection) of Jesus part of the divine δεῖ (Mark 8.31 and parallels; 9.31 and parallels; 10.34 and parallels). A notable pointer to the all-embracing significance of the raising of Jesus—in specific association with his death on the cross—is given by the account, occurring only in Matthew, of Matt. 27.52f. which tells of the raising of 'the saints who were asleep' in Jerusalem.

More detailed discussions of the significance of the raising of Jesus for the faith of primitive Christianity in Jesus Christ are to be found above all in other New Testament writings.

III

In all the New Testament writings which refer to the resurrection of Jesus, this event is associated with, and is decisive for, the saving action[38] (or at least with salvation, insofar as it is associated with a single person, cf. above on Acts[39]). This connexion is nowhere so clear, however, nor related to the whole drama of salvation in so many ways, as in Paul. Before we discuss I Cor. 15.12ff., as promised at the beginning of the essay, we will turn to a series of isolated Pauline statements and shorter passages.

With great brevity, giving the effect almost of a set formula, Paul applies the word ὑπέρ to the resurrection of Jesus in II Cor. 5.15: 'who for their sake died and was raised'; 'for their sake'

---

[38] For Rev. cf. 2.8; 1.18 (cf. Traugott Holz, *Die Christologie der Apokalypse des Johannes* [1962], p. 88) and the passages concerning the lamb that was slain, esp. 5.9, 12. For the wording of Rev. 2.8 cf. Rom. 14.9a; on this passage cf. n. 45 below. The wording in Rev. 2.8 has the form of a title of Christ (added in the form of a relative clause), and the same is the case in 1.15 (the second of the three is meant).

[39] Cf. Rengstorf, pp. 63ff., 'Das theologische Gewicht der Auferstehung Jesu', esp. pp. 63-69.

means 'for their good'. That 'raised' is not merely added here in passing is shown by Rom. 8.34, where it is explicitly added to 'died' in a formula which gives it greater prominence: no one can judge Christians, because Christ exists as he who died (vicariously) on the cross, or rather, as he who was raised (and exalted; cf. below). Elsewhere, the raising of Jesus is directly associated with the saving act in justification: Jesus was 'put to death for our trespasses and raised for our justification' (Rom. 4.25, at the end of a long passage, with great emphasis, and as a definite summary). The basis of justification as a reconstituting of human life and existence as a whole is not only the death of Jesus (in the context of the overcoming of guilt, which took place through his death in our stead), but also—as the beginning of a new existence constituted by God—in the resurrection of Jesus (the link between the two will later be considered more precisely). Paul can therefore sum this up in Rom. 10.9: 'If you believe in your heart that God raised him (Jesus) from the dead, you will be saved' (at the final judgment; salvation as a present gift is itself an eschatological act; cf. v. 10).

That the resurrection cannot be separated from the death of Jesus is made clear in the complex of statements concerning baptism in Rom. 6, which are directly related to the cross and the resurrection. In the first place, we see that the significance of ἐτάφη in I Cor. 15.4 is confirmed in Rom. 6.4; the burial as it were completes the death; but here the clause has come to be associated with the burial of the baptismal candidate in baptism, which brings about his dying with Christ on the cross. In Rom. 6.3ff. 'buried' likewise joins death and resurrection together. Just as the death of the old man (v. 6a)—as his release from the dominion of sin (v. 6b. 7)—in Rom. 6 is related to the cross of Jesus, so the new life of the Christian is directly related to the raising of Christ (and brought into association with baptism, v. 4: ἵνα . . .). Here the resurrection of Christ becomes important through the fact that the new life of Christians is constituted by it. I am of the opinion that the idea is clearly continued into vv. 5f.;[40] in their

----

[40] For more detail, cf. G. Delling, *Die Taufe im Neuen Testament*, pp. 127-31. For εἰ . . . ἀλλά in general cf. R. Kühner and B. Gerth, *Ausführliche Grammatik der griechischen Sparche*, II. 2, 4th ed. (1955), § 534 n. 6, p. 287; there it is shown that ἀλλά in the apodosis can signify a confirmation (Xenophon, *Cyrop.* I.3, 6). In Rom. 6.5 ἀλλὰ καί is not simply used in a sense identical with that of ποσῳ μᾶλλον, but in the first instance implies a correspondence: then we will in fact

new existence Christians (already) partake in the resurrection of Jesus. But even if one sought to interpret vv. 5f. differently (which is scarcely tenable exegetically), the fact that Rom. 6.4 is related to the present way of life (. . . περιπατήσωμεν) of Christians cannot be overlooked. Its newness is based upon the raising of Christ.

Here we may also mention the relationship between the receiving of a good conscience and the resurrection of Jesus which is mentioned in I Peter 3.21.

There is a specific link between the substance of those passages, which occur in different sections of the Epistle to the Romans. We have no need to discuss it separately, because it can be clearly seen in the passage I Cor. 15.12ff.; the verses we have mentioned assist us to understand I Cor. 15.12ff., and at the same time are illuminated in their turn by I Cor. 15.12ff.

The argument of this passage is unquestionably aimed against the assertion—made by a group in Corinth (τινές v. 12b)—that there is no resurrection of the dead (vv. 12b, 13a); the dead[41] will not be raised (four times: the end of v. 15; vv. 16a, 29, 32). Both formulae are equated. The group of Corinthians in question simply reject the idea of the resurrection of the dead (cf. ὅλως v. 29), with one exception: the raising of Christ is clearly not included in this rejection (special conceptions were clearly associated with the heavenly *kyrios*).

Paul opposes this by beginning with the inseparable link between the resurrection of the dead and the raising of Christ (which is why he gives the evidence for the latter in vv. 1-11). The importance of this link for Paul is obvious from a number of other epistles. Statements there show that for him the raising of Christians follows necessarily from the raising of Christ: Rom. 8.11; II Cor. 4.14; I Thess. 4.14; I Cor. 6.14, and I believe also Phil. 3.10f. The direct connexion between the two events follows from the fact that resurrection is an eschatological event (belong-

---

in the same way be incorporated into the image of his resurrection. In fact εἰ . . . ἀλλά occurs in an affirmative sense in Paul only in Rom. 6.5; the adversative usage is more usual (I Cor. 9.2; II Cor. 4.16; 5.16; 11.6; Col. 2.5; and elsewhere in the New Testament Mark 14.29). Paul speaks in other terms of the relationship between the resurrection body of Jesus and that of Christians, cf. below. On the unequivocal reference of Rom. 6.5 to the present participation of the Christian in the 'saving reality of the death and resurrection of Christ' cf. J. Schneider, *TWNT* V, pp. 194f.

[41] For νεκροί = *the* dead cf. Bauer/Arndt-Gingrich (see n. 22), s.v.

ing to the final age). The raising of Jesus inaugurates the resurrection of the dead, and furthermore, it guarantees the latter for Christians: the risen Jesus is the πρωτότοκος ἐκ τῶν νεκρῶν (Col. 1.18; cf. Rom. 8.29).[42] The form of the close association of the two acts according to Paul can also be seen in I Cor. 15.20, 23: Christ is raised from the dead as the first of those who have fallen asleep; each will be brought to life in his order: Christ as the first, and then those who belong to him, at the *parousia*. But the connexion between the two processes is far from being merely formal; both form part of the whole process of salvation, as the decisive acts which carry it out.[43] This process is concerned, as is shown, for example, by I Cor. 15.45-49, with the setting up of a new humanity, of which Christ is the first-fruits (cf. Rom. 5.12ff.). The new humanity is perfected in the (future) resurrection. This is the revealing of the full adoption of Christians as sons of God (Rom. 8.19, 21, 23).

That the raising of Jesus likewise has a christological significance for Paul can be seen (cf. below for Gal. 1.16), for example, in the credal sentence Rom. 1.4, which he presumably received as a tradition: 'designated the Son of God in power', on the basis of the resurrection of the dead, which begins with him. As the one who has been raised from the dead, he receives the title 'Lord' (Rom. 4.24; 10.9; II Cor. 4.14). It is only as the risen Christ that he can work as the Lord in his Church (Rom. 1.4f.; cf. 8.34), and only so can he bring about the consummation (I Thess. 1.10).

In I Cor. 15.13 Paul[44] draws the consequences of denying the future resurrection of the dead and the raising of Christ; if the former does not take place, neither did the latter. Without the raising of Christ, the event of salvation no longer exists. And this

---

[42] Cf. Rev. 1.5 cf. Rengstorf p. 93; W. Michaelis, *TWNT* VI, pp. 878f. From Paul's point of view, there is clearly no tension, for this particular reason, between the intention of I Cor. 15.1-11 and v. 15 (as is suggested by Braun, pp. 200ff. [cf. n. 29 above], because he understands the raising of Christ only as the first stage in an eschatological action.

[43] The essential connexion between 'the resurrection and the future of Christ' is fully discussed in the extensive third chapter of Jürgen Moltmann, *Theologie der Hoffnung* (1964); ET, *Theology of Hope* (1967).

[44] That Paul's argumentation in this passage proceeds solely (or even only primarily) from the doctrine of the resurrection in Jewish apocalyptic (to which he does not limit himself), is improbable in the context of Pauline theology and of this particular passage. The validity of the *kerygma* is not dependent upon the Jewish dogma of the resurrection—which is clearly familiar to Paul and accepted by him—but upon God's action in Christ.

is not only because the Church would then have no *kyrios*; in this context Paul makes no reference to this[45] (we must once again note that in the whole twofold passage I Cor. 15.2-22 only the title 'Christ' is used, which in Paul always signifies primarily the crucified and risen Jesus). Paul is speaking rather of the event of salvation as a whole which has taken place in Christ, and which is the whole subject of Christian preaching.

Paul begins his detailed discussion with the κήρυγμα, the proclamation of the event of the resurrection (vv. 12 and 14). Here κήρυγμα clearly represents for him the announcement of an event (cf. in the case of the cross, I Cor. 1.23) which is understood by him as a saving action of God (II Cor. 1.19), interpreted certainly, but validly interpreted, and interpreted as valid. The validity of the proclamation and interpretation—which Paul for his part regards as one and the same[46]—is something firmly established for him; it is directly rooted in God's act, which with regard to the resurrection is confirmed by the witnesses to the appearances of the risen Jesus, and is made known through a reliable tradition, which cannot be separated from the proclamation of it (I Cor. 15.1-3, 11; Gal. 2.2). With regard to the first point, Paul refers to himself as a witness of God, that is, as one who bears witness to God's act (I Cor. 16.15; God himself bears witness by Paul's preaching, [2.1 f.], he confirms the testimony of Paul as valid [1.6]). Paul says of his preaching (hardly of his preaching alone; he says 'our proclamation') that it would simply be empty, without content and without effect,[47] if Christ had not been raised (15.14). It follows necessarily, that the same would then also be true of the faith of those who receive the preaching; your faith (in which the proclamation becomes effective; the same order—proclamation, then faith—is already found in v. 11;

[45] This is done at length in Rom. 14.9a; the wording is the equivalent to that in Rom. 14.9b. (cf. II. Cor. 13.4); it does not occur in this form (in the aorist) elsewhere in Paul.

[46] Instead of this (but without the words being simply the same in meaning) Paul can also say εὐαγγέλιον, cf. especially Gal. 1.11; I Cor. 15.1; cf. Gal. 2.2, 5; Rom. 1.16, or μαρτύριον, I Cor. 2.1, cf. 1.6. On the above cf. Oscar Cullmann, *Heil als Geschichte* (1965), pp. 80-96: 'Ereignis und Deutung im Neuen Testament', esp. pp. 80f.; ET, *Salvation in History* (1967), pp. 97-114. Cf. also C. H. Dodd, *History and the Gospel* (1938), pp. 107f.

[47] Cf. e.g. Henrik Ljungman, *Pistis*. A study of its presuppositions and its meaning in Pauline Use', *Acta Soc. Human. Litt. Lundensis* 64 (1964), pp. 65f.; on I Cor. 15. pp. 55-79.

cf. the similar sequence in v. 2; the second is determined by the first) would also be empty. The purpose of this judgment becomes evident in vv. 17f.: 'your faith is futile, and you are still in your sins' (i.e. imprisoned by your sinful desire),[48] and even those who died 'in Christ' would in reality be lost (aorist—the judgment is already valid).

The two phrases complement and interpret each other in what they denote. We have already suggested that ἀπώλοντο refers to the ultimate exclusion from salvation (cf. Rom. 2.12; I Cor. 1.18, etc.; Phil. 1.28—the opposite is to be redeemed). 'In Christ' signifies here, as frequently elsewhere, that one's destiny is decided through the crucified (and risen) Christ: those who die trusting in God's redeeming action in Christ, if Christ had not been raised, would be subject to judgment (v. 18; cf. v. 2 δι' οὗ καὶ σώζεσθε, and the context). V. 17 emphasizes that Christians would still be prey to the force of evil-doing (or else that, in the conventional sense, the guilt of Christians would not be done away with): your destiny would then still be determined by (or in) your sins (and of course for Paul the dominion of sin over man is always and in any case taken away in the cross of Jesus, Rom. 6.6b, 7). Thus the cross of Christ is not a real saving act without the resurrection.

What we previously deduced from the Epistle to the Romans shows that this does not simply mean that the resurrection of Christ confirms the cross as willed by God, ratifying it as God's act. According to I Cor. 15.17 there is in fact no redemption from man's fallen condition without the resurrection of Christ as an event brought about by God—liberation from existence in sin is based upon the crucified and risen Christ. We are reminded of Rom. 4.25: Christ was raised for the sake of our justification (cf. Rom. 8.34; II Cor. 5.15). Without the resurrection of Christ, there would be no reconstituting of human life and existence by God, and the whole of man's life and existence is always implied here. Liberation from subjection to sin (or sins) is for Paul, and in the context of the saving action of God towards man, inseparable from making it possible for man 'to walk in a new way'; here we

---

[48] Cf. for this interpretation of the plural n. 6 above, on Rom. 7.5. Jeremias (cf. n. 6 above), p. 96 (ET, p. 101), thinks of I Cor. 15.7 as a 'later effect of the *kerygma*' presumably produced by v. 3. Braun (cf. n. 29 above) interprets I Cor. 15.17 (in accordance with Rom. 7.14) of concrete actual sins.

are reminded of Rom. 6.4f. (cf. v. 6). Col. 2.12f., forming an exact parallel in its content to Rom. 6.5b states that Christians are raised with Christ ($X\rho\iota\sigma\tau\acute{o}s$, v. 11) and are made alive with him (cf. the basis given for the parenesis in 3.1). Paul lives with the risen Christ through the power of God, which was mightily exercised in the raising of Christ (II Cor. 13.4; $X\rho\iota\sigma\tau\acute{o}s$, v. 3).

IV

According to the statements of the New Testament, the faith of primitive Christianity regarded the raising of Jesus as the decisive act of God's saving work. It has a key position in this, in a very precise sense. It is through the raising of Jesus that God once and for all identifies the whole earthly ministry of Jesus as the work of him who inaugurates the kingdom of God by his preaching and actions, and by his words and acts redeems men and brings them into the kingdom of God; God confirms by raising Jesus that his actions were carried out under God's command, and were God's actions.[49] If the saving action of the earthly Jesus is con-

[49] Cf. Wilckens, *Offenbarung* pp. 6of.; Pannenberg, *Christologie*, pp. 6of., 261 and especially §3. Wilckens seeks to interpret the resurrection of Jesus in the framework 'of the primitive Christian faith in the risen Christ' as above all 'the final confirmation by God, which has already taken place, of the claim of Jesus', as 'the divine ratification of the claim which Jesus put forward in everything he said and did—especially in his unqualified promise of eschato-logical salvation' (*Offenbarung*, p. 61). But Wilckens believes that the text allows him to say 'with great certainty' that 'Jesus . . . himself must have taken into account the possibility of his death' (*Offenbarung*, p. 60). But the question then arises whether Jesus saw his death—'as the divinely willed conclusion of his ministry' (*ibid*. on the basis of Luke 13.31-33)—only from the point of view that God (after and beyond his death) 'would demonstrate the truth of his claim by what was destined to happen to him' (*op. cit.*, p. 61); that is, whether this link between the death and resurrection of Jesus (for which cf. in particular the missionary sermons of Acts), provides an adequate inter-pretation. Though Wilckens first hesitantly suggests that Jesus may have taken into account the *possibility* of his violent death as divinely willed, he goes on at once to say that Jesus obviously 'himself sought a clash with the authori-ties' (*Offenbarung*, p. 60, cf. Pannenberg, *Christologie*, p. 60) and that he brought 'the clash to a head in the belief . . . that God would demonstrate by what was destined to happen to him the truth of his claim' (*Offenbarung*, p. 61). This implies that Jesus assumed the *necessity* of his violent death; but 'necessity' implies the question of a specific meaning for his death, and includes the $\delta\epsilon\hat{\iota}$, which is characteristic of the divinely willed events of the end of the age. (The fact that the prophecies of the passion to some extent already manifest the specific features of the passion narrative—especially in Mark 10.33f. and parallels—does not necessarily exclude Jesus' having spoken in some form of the death that faced him, cf. for the form, the short

summated by his death, by raising him God places his seal on the facts that Jesus went to the cross in obedience to God's will, and that in giving up his Son to death God acted to save.[50] Indeed at the same time the event of the resurrection reveals to primitive Christianity the mystery of the person of Jesus[51] as that of the Son sent by God, who in his work carried out the saving purpose of God, that is, in his work as he who (in free obedience) was humbled and (by God) was exalted. The raising of Jesus is the prerequisite for the work of the exalted Christ,[52] which is consummated in the *parousia* and in the events which this sets into motion (cf. I Cor. 15.23-28 in its context). The resurrection as an eschatological event reveals Jesus as the first member of a new humanity. It is the beginning of the new creation and the pledge of its consummation. Through it Christians already partake in (new) life (Paul; cf. the Gospel of John), and it determines the whole life and existence of Christians—making it eschatological.

It is important that we should give a brief exposition of the statement that the event of the resurrection reveals the mystery of the person of Jesus to primitive Christianity—in the context of his work, it must be noted. We turn to two passages, which in the literary sense are the earliest and the latest texts to show this. Paul speaks of the manifestation of the risen Christ which was

---

version in Luke 9.44, but especially, for the substance, Mark 10.45 and parallels).

[50] This understanding of the raising of Jesus goes wholly beyond all Jewish analogies. This is also basically true of our previous sentence, although one can still compare it to Jewish statements concerning the resurrection of the just to eternal life, such as, for example, Ps. Sal. 3.12b: 'Those who fear the Lord will rise to eternal life' (cf. E. Lohse, *RGG* 3rd ed. I, col. 694; a fuller collection of material is found in Strack-Billerbeck, *Kommentar zum Neuen Testament aus Talmud und Midrasch*, IV (1928), pp. 1166-98; for Josephus cf. pp. 1188f.); similarly according to Josephus B.J. 2. 163 the ἀγαθοί will receive 'another body'—in 3.374 he mentions the ἁγνά σώματα which they receive; according to *contra Apionem* 2.218 those who are faithful to the *torah* will receive 'a better life' (the statements all refer to the final resurrection), etc. (the New Testament mentions the resurrection of the righteous in Luke 14.14). In Acts 3.14 the resurrection of Jesus is in fact referred to as the raising of the Righteous One by God (cf. the title of the Righteous One given to him who appeared to Paul in 22.14). But there is decisive evidence in the statements of the New Testament concerning the raising of Jesus of the unique significance of the events of the resurrection, within the equally unique saving act of God in Christ in general.

[51] Cf. for example Hugh Anderson, *Jesus and Christian Origins* (1964).

[52] Rom. 8.34; Eph. 1.20; Acts 2.32f. (οὖν v. 33.; 5.30f.; I Peter 1.21, cf. 3.21f., cf. pp. 90ff. above), obviously a familiar theme.

vouchsafed to him, that God revealed his Son to him (Gal. 1.16; for the inclusion of the title 'Son' cf. I Thess. 1.10): until then he had judged Jesus κατὰ σάρκα, by human standards (II Cor. 5.16); in the risen Jesus he recognized the Son—who for Paul is above all the one in whom the love of God is made known in its entirety, by God's sending the one who is uniquely close to himself into the world, and giving him on the cross for the redemption of mankind (cf., for example, Rom. 8.32); but from now on the Son has been installed in power (Rom. 1.4; cf. above). In the Gospel of John, the appearance of the risen Jesus to the doubting Thomas not only convinces him of the identity of him who has appeared with the crucified Jesus (20.27), but provokes the confession of faith which can be regarded as the highest confession of all the utterances recorded in the Gospel of John: 'My Lord and my God' (v. 28). The title κύριος cannot simply be taken, on account of the word μου which is added ('My Lord') as a mere identification with the earthly Jesus who was called 'Lord' by the disciples, but can only be understood as a complete confession of faith in the Lord of the Church; the title θεός goes beyond everything that was said about the earthly Jesus (and indeed also beyond everything that can be said of him according to John) and points back to the prologue, and therefore to the pre-existent Son, to which exalted status, as it was before his earthly ministry, Jesus is now restored through the resurrection (John 17.5). Even in the gospel tradition outside John the key position of the event of the resurrection for faith in Jesus Christ is evident. It is particularly clear in the Gospel of Mark that the disciples' understanding of the work and person of Jesus before the resurrection is very limited. In Mark this fact is elaborated in a special way, with particular regard to the person of Jesus, into a kind of theory of the Messianic secret (whereas in Matthew and Luke their failure to understand is to some extent played down).[53] This does not in any way lead to the conclusion that the characteristics of the Christ of faith were simply imposed upon the portrait of Jesus by the post-resurrection Church.[54] But it was there nevertheless

---

[53] Cf. Erik Sjöberg, 'Der verborgene Menschensohn in den Evangelien', *Acta Soc. Human. Litt. Lund.* 53, 1955, and my review in *TL* 83, 1958, cols. 422-6; also Anderson (cf. n. 51 above), pp. 243-7 on Mark and pp. 247-253 on Matthew.

[54] Cf. R. Bultmann, *Theologie des Neuen Testaments*, 3rd ed. (1959), pp. 33f. ET, *Theology of the New Testament*, i (1952), pp. 35f.

that the understanding of the work and person of Jesus was in fact first obtained. This can also be seen in Mark in the fact that he only uses the title 'Jesus Christ', which sums up in itself the post-resurrection faith in Christ of the Church, at the beginning of his gospel (1.1; the formula in 9.41 falls outside the framework which the rest of Mark maintains; otherwise χριστός occurs there only in the sense of the concept of the Messiah: 8.29; 12.35; 13.21; 14.61; 15.32). It is also clear from the way in which the statements of Jesus concerning the Son of man remain largely beyond the disciples' understanding. The upheaval which the event of the resurrection brought to Jesus' followers is mentioned by Mark at the close of the narrative of the empty tomb (16.8). We are reminded of the verses in the Gospel of John which explicitly tell how the disciples were not able to understand the precise significance of words and acts of Jesus until after the resurrection (2.22; 12.16, at the entry into Jerusalem); in 16.23 the disciples are explicitly told, with regard to the fellowship with Jesus which is to be renewed through the resurrection:[55] 'In that day you will ask me no questions.' They are promised that the resurrection will bring them full knowledge (cf. also 14.26).

Our contention that a true understanding of the work and person of Jesus was only vouchsafed to the disciples (as the 'first-fruits' of primitive Christianity) through his resurrection does not mean that we are suggesting that the saving significance of the work and person of Jesus itself has its origin in the disciples' belief in the resurrection as such. According to the New Testament, this is given by the act of God. Accordingly, the origin of the faith of the disciples in the resurrection is also to be sought in the act of God, in raising and manifesting the risen Jesus.

But following the New Testament, we can only make this statement in the manner of the κήρυγμα, or of the confession of faith,[56] bearing in mind that κήρυγμα is the valid proclamation of an event. Just as to a certain extent the work and person of Jesus is accessible to the pure historian by virtue of the statements of the

---

[55] C. K. Barrett, *The Gospel According to St John*, 1955, says (with reference to 16.23) of the parallel 14.20, that 'the primary reference is to the resurrection'. A. Schlatter, *Der Evangelist Johannes*, also takes 16.23 of the resurrection. For what proceeds above and follows cf. also Cullmann (cf. n. 46 above), pp. 85-87; ET 102-4).

[56] Cf. pp. 80ff., 97 above.

synoptic gospels in particular (in my view to a greater extent than it is often allowed at the present time), so it is also possible for him to recognize that to a certain extent the substance of the disciples' belief in the resurrection is associated with the work and person of Jesus, and likewise it is possible for him to acknowledge that faith in the risen Jesus is associated with particular experiences on the part of the disciples.[57] But the pure historian cannot tell whether God is acting in the work of Jesus, and whether the faith in the resurrection, which is due to certain experiences, derives from an act of God (however incapable he may be of denying it). However, I do not see in this any adequate cause for the theologian to reject the well-founded statement that the origin of the disciples' faith in the resurrection is to be found in God's act in raising and manifesting Jesus (and therefore I do not see anything which should cause the theologian to identify himself with the pure historian; I do not see how this would make him any more worthy of belief).

As we have seen from several passages, the certainty of primitive Christianity[58] that its faith in the resurrection has its origin in God's act in raising Jesus derives from the statements of the witnesses to the appearances of the risen Christ. The first generation of primitive Christianity, in Jerusalem (cf. Acts 2.32; 3.15; 4.33; cf. above), in Caesarea (Acts 10.41), and in Corinth (I Cor. 15.11), with the exception of the witnesses to the resurrection themselves already depended upon their statements. And in fact they depended almost from the first not merely on the direct testimony of those to whom they had been vouchsafed, but upon the preaching of those who in their turn depended upon the testimony of the witnesses to the resurrection (cf. Acts 13.31).[59] (The possibility mentioned in I Cor. 15.6 of questioning the witnesses of the resurrection themselves does not alter what has been said; this possibility was in any case not unlimited.) Even Paul derives the gospel of the raising of Jesus from the statements of such witnesses as Peter, James, the twelve etc. (I Cor. 15.5-7). At a

---

[57] Cf. e.g. Pannenberg, *Christologie*, pp. 95-97.

[58] What follows is what must in my view be argued against the suggestions of W. Marxsen, 'Die Auferstehung Jesus als historisches und theologisches Problem' 2nd ed. (1965); ET, pp. 15-50 above. Cf. with the argument above Cullmann (see n. 46 above), pp. 80f.; 84f. ET, 97f., 101f. Grass, pp. 257f., 260.

[59] The author of Acts does not allow Paul to appeal here to the ὤφθη which he had experienced.

very early stage this testimony was handed down through the links in a chain of tradition.

Therefore from the first it was the preaching of all of those who proclaimed the gospel of Christ—their preaching deriving of course from the statements of the witnesses to the resurrection and appearing to them—which testified to the resurrection of Jesus[60]—on the basis, of course, of the received testimony of those to whom the resurrection appearances had been vouchsafed. We must mention again that Paul derives the faith of the Corinthians in the raising of Jesus from the preaching of the missionaries (I Cor. 15.11; cf. κηρύσσεται v. 12). We saw that preaching means in this case, as with regard to the cross, the proclamation of a fact or an event. By the proclamation carried out by those whom he had sent, God brings about faith in the raising of Jesus from the dead (Rom. 10.15, 14, 9; here the process is set out in reverse order), through which redemption is given (v. 9; cf. above). The verbal character of the preaching does not permit us to overlook the fact that the preaching (I Cor. 2.4, cf. 4.20, κενόν 15.14), and what is preached itself has the nature of an event. The certainty of the raising of Jesus—which is decisive for faith in Christ (I Cor. 15.12ff., etc.)—is based upon the word which hands on the statements of the witnesses to the resurrection, validly interprets the event of the resurrection in terms of its saving significance, and is received as the word of God (I Thess. 2.13). In the 'word of God'—which is why it is known as such—God himself bears testimony to his saving work in the raising of Jesus Christ; that is, in the word which is handed on by men.

[60] On the close link between tradition and preaching in Paul, cf. Rengstorf, p. 86.

IV

Hans-Georg Geyer

THE RESURRECTION OF JESUS CHRIST: A SURVEY OF THE DEBATE IN PRESENT DAY THEOLOGY

IF the message of an Easter sermon is merely that someone who regards Good Friday as the greatest festival is ultimately, be it with sorrow or with rejoicing, only celebrating the burial of God, it is presenting in the most acute form possible the theological problem of the resurrection. For such an idea betrays an abstract antithesis between the cross and the resurrection of Jesus Christ, according to which the crucifixion is nothing more than the assault of forces hostile to God, whereas, by direct contrast, the resurrection is the act of the love of God, the power of which to give life is infinitely greater than the force of death in the world.

The question whether this conception of the cross and resurrection of Jesus Christ, in the form of a contradictory opposition between the evil inclination of the world towards death and the righteous will of God for life, is justified, is a question which indicates the primary problem of the theme of the resurrection. It does not consist of the question which largely dominates present day discussion, that of the fact of the resurrection, and whether it actually took place in space and time. The question of the significance of the resurrection of Jesus Christ must be regarded as the primary problem. For the question of fact is only meaningful as a consequence of the question of its significance, while the problem of the significance of the resurrection of Jesus, if rightly understood, can only be that of its meaning in its original context. And there is no dispute among theologians that the resurrection of Jesus cannot be seen as an isolated problem. The differences are rather over what the original context is, in which the event, or the assertion, of the resurrection of Jesus Christ has its basic significance. With regard to this problem one can distinguish three main approaches in present day theological discussion, which, although they overlap in individual details, are distinct in ways which are not obscured by this overlapping. The first approach is that represented by Rudolf Bultmann and Karl Barth, insofar as both regard the context which constitutes the meaning of the resurrection of Jesus Christ as lying in its relationship to the cross. The second approach is that represented by Willi Marxsen and Gerhardt Ebeling; for them the decisive and defining context for the event of the resurrection is formed by going back to the words and deeds of the historical Jesus. Finally, the third approach is presented by Ulrich Wilckens and Wolfhart Pannenberg, in the thesis that the system of reference which is fundamental in constituting the significance of the resurrection of Christ is to be sought in the apocalyptic expectation of the general resurrection of the dead and the judgment at the end of the world.

I

A. In his lectures in the spring of 1935 on the Apostles' Creed, Karl Barth notes at the beginning of his exposition of the words in the second article of the Creed, *crucifixus, mortuus et sepultus*:

Having characterized the second Article as the centre of the whole Creed, we shall have to call the clauses that deal with the *death* and the *resurrection* of Jesus Christ the centre within this centre. The work of New Testament exegesis shows no clearer result than this: that from all sides the witness of the Apostles and Evangelists pours in upon this centre; *crucifixus est et resurrexit*. Here all the threads of Christian knowledge run together, visibly or invisibly. It is from here that the significance for the Christian Credo of the Incarnation, the Second Coming, and even of Creation or of the Church is to be guarded. It is here, therefore, that the spirits are separated.[1]

As far as the link between the assertions concerning the death and the resurrection of Jesus Christ are concerned, which according to Karl Barth's judgment form the 'centre within the centre' in the Creed, the spirits of Barth and Bultmann at least are not distinguished in this point. For Bultmann also considers that in the

[1] K. Barth, Credo. *Die Hauptprobleme der Dogmatik, dargestellt im Anschluss an das Apostolische Glaubensbekenntnis*, sixteen lectures delivered at the University of Utrecht in February and March 1935, (1935), p. 75 (ET, *Credo: A presentation of the Chief Problems of Dogmatics with Reference to the Apostles' Creed* [1936]), p. 85. English translations (when available) were used here and elsewhere.

question of the constituting and making possible of Christian faith, as the true form of existential life for man, through the event of Christ, 'the crux of the matter lies in the cross and the resurrection',[2] as he expresses it in his essay 'Neues Testament und Mythologie' (The New Testament and Mythology) of 1941.

Without going into the matter in greater detail Bultmann localizes the event of salvation in a strict sense in the cross of Jesus Christ; the starting point, accepted without question, of Bultmann's consideration of the theme of the revelation of the love of God in Jesus Christ, which is the basis of faith, is that the cross is to be regarded as a saving event.

When the New Testament exalts 'the historical event of the cross' to 'cosmic dimensions' (cf. e.g. Col. 2.13-15), it is here simply expressing the 'significance (of the cross) as a historical event' (p. 42, ET, p. 36). For that judgment has come upon the 'world' through the cross of Christ, means that 'the cross becomes the judgment of ourselves as fallen creatures enslaved to the powers of the "world" ' (*ibid.*). Thus 'to believe in the cross' should be taken to mean 'to make the cross of Christ our own, to undergo crucifixion with him' (*ibid.*). To this extent the saving event is 'not an isolated incident which befell a mythical personage' (*ibid.*) but an act of God which overturns, as well as establishes, the basis of human life, because it is effective as an eschatological event; that is, 'the cross is not just an event of the past which can be contemplated, but is an eschatological event in and beyond time, insofar as it [understood in its significance, that is, for faith] is an ever-present reality' (*ibid.*).

The cross of Jesus Christ as an eschatological saving event and as the content of faith is 'a fact which is claimed to take place within and to effect the course of history, and which originates from the concrete and verifiable event of the crucifixion of Jesus' (p. 43, cf. ET, p. 37). In this 'historical' significace, it is 'the judgment of the world, the judgment and the deliverance of man' (*ibid.*), that is, the judgment of divine grace pronounced over the whole world and therefore affecting every human being, liberating man from himself as a being belonging to the world, and setting him free to be a being belonging to God.

[2] R. Bultmann, 'Neues Testament und Mythologie, in *Offenbarung und Heilsgeschehen* (Beitr. zur Ev. Theol. vol. 7, 1941). This essay is quoted from the reprint in *Kerygma und Mythos* I, ed. H. W. Bartsch, 2nd (unaltered) ed. (1951), p. 41. (ET, *Kerygma and Myth*, trans. R. H. Fuller [1961], p. 35.)

The assertion that the cross of Jesus Christ is the eschatological saving event necessarily provokes the epistemological criticism which Bultmann presents very simply in the form of a question: 'Is this significance to be discerned in the actual event of past history?' (*ibid.*). This presumably means: is the knowledge of the universal saving significance of the cross of Jesus Christ a meaningful problem for the historical study of the crucifixion of Jesus of Nazareth? If this were the case, the interpretation of the cross as the historical saving event which it is for faith would have to be derived from the course of Jesus' life, as it can be reconstructed in historical terms. The ministry of the historical Jesus, his preaching and what he said and did, with all its historical implications, would then have to contain within itself the necessary prerequisites and an adequate basis for the understanding of the saving significance of his suffering and death. Bultmann expresses this by asking: 'If we are to perceive the real meaning of the cross, must we understand it as the cross of Jesus as a figure of past history? Must we go back to the Jesus of history?' (p. 43, ET, p. 38).

For two reasons Bultmann regards this hypothetical possibility as a pure fiction. First, because at best it was realizable only for 'the first preachers of the gospel'. 'For them the cross was the cross of him with whom they had lived in personal intercourse. The cross was an experience of their own lives. It presented them with a question and it disclosed to them its meaning' (*ibid.*). But for all other men, who had not lived in direct contact with the historical Jesus as his contemporaries, 'this personal connexion cannot be reproduced' (pp. 43f., ET, pp. 38f.) the crucifixion of Jesus also does not form part of their own living experience, so that it is not possible for their personal experience of the earthly Jesus to become the basis of the re-experiencing of his crucifixion in their own existential life.

Secondly, Bultmann emphasizes that 'the New Testament does not proclaim Jesus Christ in this way (i.e. the meaning of the cross is derived from historical report)'. The meaning of the cross is not disclosed from the life of Jesus as a figure of past history, a life which needs to be reproduced by historical research. On the contrary, Jesus is not proclaimed merely as the crucified; he is also risen from the dead (p. 44, ET, p. 38). This statement is anything but a passing remark; in it Bultmann is formulating a basic theological principle of the widest relevance, which he goes on at once to re-express in very precise terms: 'The cross and the resurrection form an inseparable unity' (*ibid.*). In Bultmann's sense, this statement has an exclusive connotation with regard to the cross of Jesus Christ, in that the latter can be understood as God's eschatological act of salvation only when taken together with the resurrection, just as it signifies for the resurrection that its original meaning is in essence comprehended in its unity with the cross.

Thus Bultmann's theology states unambiguously that the affirmation of the unity of the cross and resurrection of Jesus Christ, as the original context of the saving significance of the cross, implies a denial that the unity between the life and death, ministry and passion, preaching and crucifixion of Jesus form the context which constitutes and provides the eschatological significance of the cross of Jesus Christ. But it is far from unequivocal in expounding this unity, as a theological axiom, with regard to the factor of the resurrection in it. The difficulties result from the problem of adequately defining the nature of the statements concerning the resurrection of Christ contained in the New Testament tradition. For—a further point in which Bultmann and Barth agree—obviously 'it (that is, the resurrection of Jesus Christ as it is affirmed) is not an event of past history with a self-evident meaning' (*ibid.*).

With this negative assumption, Bultmann sees himself forced to accept that 'the resurrection narratives and every other mention of the resurrection' is nothing more than 'an attempt to convey the meaning of the cross' (*ibid.*). That is, in formal terms, the assertion of the resurrection is not a judgment upon reality, which sets out in words, that is, in a form accessible to all, a state of affairs independent of the subject who passes this judgment (regardless of whether the state of affairs affects the subject in the sphere of knowledge alone or in the ontological sphere). Instead, it is a reflective judgment in which the subject which makes the judgment recognizes an effect which it has experienced from something outside itself (regardless of whether this is a state of affairs in space and time, or a meaningful concept set out in words), and goes on to describe how this effect is possible, that is, it describes the significance of whatever it is for all possible subjects. The reflective judgment upon the resurrection of Jesus

Christ expresses and implies the admonition 'that his death is not just an ordinary human death, but the judgment and salvation of the world, depriving death of its power' (*ibid.*).

Here Bultmann has drawn the cross and the resurrection of Jesus Christ into an inseparable unity which one might refer to, in the words of Fuchs, as the language-event of the cross, insofar as the resurrection of Jesus Christ is the putting into words of the cross of Jesus Christ as God's eschatological bringing of salvation. In material terms, the cross and resurrection of Jesus Christ form the two contrary aspects, complementary, however, in their opposition, of one and the same saving event, 'which brings judgment to the world and opens up for men the possibility of authentic life' (p. 44, ET, p. 39), that is, by which, together with the denial of being which is based upon the world, the assertion is made of being which is based upon God.

The fact that the cross and resurrection of Jesus Christ coincide to form one fundamental and decisive eschatological event make it quite impossible to think of the resurrection as 'a miraculous proof capable of demonstration and sufficient to convince the sceptic that the cross really has the cosmic and eschatological significance accorded to it' (*ibid.*). For, as Bultmann says in somewhat loose terms, the resurrection is 'an article of faith just as much as the meaning of the cross itself'; but he corrects himself, and the next sentence is more precise; 'Faith in the resurrection is really the same thing as faith in the saving efficacy of the cross' (p. 46, ET, p. 41).

This conclusion closes the circle which was begun with the question of how the cross of Jesus Christ could be understood as a saving event. At first, it may, perhaps, have seemed that faith in the resurrection was being regarded as something beyond the cross, which was the real source of the faith which interpreted it; but the drawing together of the cross and the resurrection into an inseparable unity radically excludes anything beyond them, and the question once again rises: 'How do we come to believe in the cross as the saving event?'

Bultmann's reply is: 'There is only one answer. This is the way in which the cross is proclaimed. It is always proclaimed together with the resurrection' (*ibid.*). This does not only mean that the expressions 'the cross as the saving event' and 'the cross together with the resurrection' are synonymous in the strictest sense, but it also has an exclusive meaning, in that the cross as the saving event, or the cross together with the resurrection (or, more briefly, the resurrection itself), exists solely when uttered in the word of preaching. 'The word of preaching confronts us as the word of God. It is not for us to question its credentials, it is we who are questioned, we who are asked whether we will believe the word or reject it' (*ibid.*). And the faith which accepts and understands the word of preaching is 'real Easter faith': it is the faith that 'the word of preaching' is the authentic 'word of God' (*ibid.*).

Just as the resurrection of Jesus Christ as the true significance of the cross of Jesus only occurs in the word of preaching, so it is this word which 'supplements the cross and makes its saving efficacy intelligible by demanding faith' (p. 47, ET, p. 42). If the saving efficacy of the cross is made present because it occurs in preaching, so the future of the cross also lies in the supplementing of the cross by the word in preaching: 'the eschatological "now" is here' in the present event of preaching, which is the future of the cross (*ibid.*).

B. Barth criticizes this conception, which appears to be extremely consistent, in his *Church Dogmatics* III 2, pp. 531ff. (ET, pp. 442ff.), but does not overlook the fact that Bultmann's exposition, by contrast with that of Kümmel and Cullmann 'at least . . . [emphasizes] the central and indispensable function of the event of Easter for all that is thought and said in the New Testament'.[3] Barth formulates this principal point of disagreement in the following sentence: 'R. Bultmann "demythologizes" the event of Easter by interpreting it as "the rise of faith in the risen Lord", since it was this faith which led to the apostolic preaching' (*Kerygma and Myth*, ET, p. 42).[4] That is, as the real object of his criticism Barth singles out the identification of the resurrection of Christ with the coming into being of faith in Jesus Christ. The circumstance that Barth aims his criticism at Bultmann's systematic assumptions, instead of exposing, by an internal criticism, the questions which Bultmann's understanding of the resurrection leaves open and unanswered, may be due to the fact that—to a certain limited extent—he oversimplifies

---

[3] K. Barth, *Die Kirchliche Dogmatik*, III: *Die Lehre von der Schöpfung*, 2; p. 531, ET, *The Doctrine of Creation* in *Church Dogmatics*, III. 2, p. 443.
[4] *Ibid.*

Bultmann's view. The full wording of the sentence in Bultmann to which Barth draws attention is: 'If the event of Easter Day is in any sense an historical event additional to the event of the cross, it is nothing else than the rise of faith in the risen Lord, since it was this faith which led to the apostolic preaching' (*Kerygma and Myth*, ET, p. 42). What Barth does not quote, but which is unquestionably essential to the meaning of Bultmann's statement, is the restricting and defining subordinate clause: 'If the event of Easter Day is in any sense a historical event additional to the event of the cross.' To this extent, but to this extent alone, the Easter event is nothing more than the rise of belief in the resurrection. Bultmann in fact goes on to make this doubly clear: 'The resurrection itself is not an event of past history. All that historical criticism can establish is the fact that the first disciples came to believe in the resurrection' (*ibid.*). In these terms, Bultmann can clearly now speak of the event of Easter Day in a double sense, in that of history, insofar as the Easter event as the rise of 'Christian belief in the resurrection' is a historical event, and in the sense of faith, where 'the event of Easter Day as the resurrection of Christ' is in no sense an historical event. Bultmann further asserts that 'the historical problem is not of interest to Christian belief in the resurrection', for to Christian faith, 'the historical event of the rise of the Easter faith', that is, the Easter event, insofar as it is still in fact accessible to historical investigation, signifies as 'for the first disciples . . . the self-attestation of the risen Lord, the act of God in which the redemptive event of the cross is completed' (*ibid.*).

With these formulae Bultmann has admittedly reached a limit which he does not transgress. But further reflection is inhibited at this point; the question remains, whether, at the point at which the historical consciousness can only record the commencement of belief in the resurrection, with the first witnesses to belief in the 'self-attestation of the risen Lord', the statement of faith concerning the 'act of God in which the redemptive event of the cross is completed' is not evidently bound to be an arbitrary one; and no further attempt is made to think out an answer to this question. Consequently, the meaning of the statement which forms the limit of Bultmann's assertion remains hidden in an unresolved ambiguity. When E. Fuchs describes Bultmann's intention as follows: 'At Easter the disciples became aware—not who he was (for then Easter would not be an eschatological event, but an event within history), but who he is',[5] the unanswered question is indirectly shown to be the 'ontological' question of theology, concerning the being of the *Christus praesens* who is the basis of faith. When faith speaks of the event of Easter Day as 'the self-attestation of the risen Lord', it is speaking of the event by which a basis is provided for faith, but by that very token not of the question of the way faith arose. It is just this difference between the providing of a basis for faith and the coming into being of faith, which is ignored and unexamined in Bultmann's view of the events of Easter, to such an extent that Barth's suspicion of the identification in principle of the resurrection of Christ and the coming into being of faith—in spite of Bultmann's restriction of this identification to the historical sphere—is a justifiable criticism.[6]

Of the axioms which Barth regards as fundamental to Bultmann's view and criticizes as such, the second is, in my view, of central importance, that is, that 'an event alleged to have happened in time can be accepted as historical only if it can be proved to be a "historical fact"' (*Church Dogmatics*, III. 2, p. 535, ET, p. 446). For a line of thought which subjects itself to this axiom, and which does not accept the resurrection of Christ as an historical datum, logically finds itself committed to two identifications which are characteristic of Bultmann's view of the events of Easter: (1) The identification of the cross and the resurrection, insofar as the unhistorical resurrection of Christ is the significance of the historical crucifixion of Jesus (the unity of the two is the unity of the event and its meaning); and (2) the identification of the resurrection of Christ and the rising of faith, insofar as in faith the significance of the cross, which constitutes the essence of the resurrection, is actualized in existential life (the unity of the two is the unity of meaning and understanding).

Again, it is as much characteristic of Barth's whole thought that the axiom of the necessary historicity of everything which occurs in space and time and happens to man, is not valid for him, as it is significant that the exclusion of this axiom is not given the status of a primary fundamental principle.

[5] E. Fuchs, 'Das entmythologisierte Glaubensärgernis', 1952, in *Zum hermeneutischen Problem in der Theologie. Die existentiale Interpretation* (1959), p. 228.   [6] Barth, *op. cit.* III. 2, pp. 534ff.; trans. pp. 446ff.

This can clearly be seen from the positive development of his doctrine of the resurrection of Jesus Christ in *Church Dogmatics* IV 1 § 59.3 ('The Verdict of the Father'); it is explained there as an answer to the question of whether, reflecting upon the judgment of God pronounced upon the world in the cross of Jesus Christ, it is right and possible to apply and transfer it to us. W. Kreck puts the question in this form: 'How is it possible for us to know that the event of the atonement in Jesus Christ is valid for us, affects us and includes us?'[7] As an adequate and compelling basis for this Barth advances the judgment of the Father carried out ontologically in the resurrection of Jesus Christ; although in expounding this positive answer[8] he makes no explicit reference to Bultmann, a profound disagreement with him is in fact noticeable in every line (cf. his Preface). With regard to the New Testament narratives of the resurrection, there is no disagreement about the fact 'that in the story which they recount we have to do with an "act of God", the act of God in which it was revealed to the disciples that the happening of the cross was the redemptive happening promised to them on which therefore the community and its message were founded' (p. 373, ET, p. 338). But for Barth this agreement concerns only the preliminaries to the understanding of Easter, which he then goes on to develop in five points in a way which considerably limits the original agreement.

1. He begins by 'stating basically that the raising of Jesus Christ (with all that it implies for us and for all men) is in the New Testament comprehended and understood as an act of God with the same seriousness as the preceding event of the cross with its implication for us and for all men' (p. 330, ET, p. 300). It is exclusively the act of God simply because, by contrast with the event of the crucifixion, it contains no 'component of human action', which in fact give to the latter an '"historical" character'; it is solely and exclusively the act of God basically because of the 'divine revelation which has taken place in this event' (pp. 331f., ET, pp. 301f.). In the resurrection, as the testimony of Jesus Christ to himself, the revelation of God which has been given by God's raising him is imparted, the knowledge that God himself

[7] W. Kreck, 'Die Lehre von der Versöhnung' (on Karl Barth, *Kirchliche Dogmatik*, Vol. IV, 1 and 2) in TL 85 (1960), col. 90.

[8] K. Barth, *Die Kirchliche Dogmatik*, IV, *Die Lehre von der Versöhnung*, 1 (1935), pp. 323ff.; ET, *The Doctrine of Reconciliation* in *Church Dogmatics*, IV. 1, pp. 294ff.

has already been at work in the life and death of Jesus Christ.

2. Under the second point, Barth specifies that [the raising of Jesus Christ] is 'an autonomous, new act of God', independent of the event of the crucifixion, and so rejects the view that it is only 'the noetic converse of it', doing no more than to bring to life the saving significance of the cross in the consciousness and life of the first disciples (p. 335, ET, p. 304). As 'an event which has its own content and form', as 'an act of God *sui generis*', that is, 'as the true and original and typical act of revelation', the event of the resurrection is distinguished by Barth from that of the crucifixion. The raising of Jesus Christ to life from death is to be contrasted with the fact of his death, as 'a free act of [God's] grace' (p. 336, ET, pp. 304-5). It 'is the great verdict of God, the fulfilment and proclamation of God's decision concerning the event of the cross' (p. 340, ET, p. 309), and as Barth calls it, his 'justification' (pp. 340f., ET, pp. 309f.) as it were of the judgment upon us, which was carried out by God himself in the crucifixion of Jesus Christ, and which brings us salvation.

While in the first point, that the resurrection of Christ is an act of revelation by God, Barth rejects the view that the act of atonement brought about in the death of Jesus Christ on the cross was substantially completed only by his resurrection, and affirms that the resurrection rather brought to light its truth and its validity, in the second point, that the raising of Jesus Christ is a separate and new act of God, he rejected the view that it is only the actualization of the knowledge of the work of redemption that preceded it, and affirms that as an event distinct from the judgment on the cross, it is the self-justification of God which underlies our acceptance by God (pp. 337f., ET, pp. 305.).

3. But the central point of his exposition is formed by the answer, given as the third point, to the question of the 'positive connexion between the death of Jesus Christ and His resurrection' (p. 341; ET, p. 309). Expressed in formal terms this is: 'the positive connexion between the death and resurrection of Jesus Christ consists in the fact that these two acts of God with and after one another are the two basic events of the one history of God with a sinful and corrupt world. His history with us as perverted and lost creatures' (p. 341, ET, p. 310). The two events which comprise the 'alteration in our situation', our reconciliation with and a return to God, have a 'differentiated relationship', in

that what took place was first 'a negative event (with a positive intention!) . . . [and] then a positive event (with a negative pre-supposition!)' (p. 342; ET, p. 310). 'According to the resurrection the death of Jesus Christ as the negative act of God took place with a positive intention. It has as its aim the turning of man to Himself, his positing afresh, his putting on of a new life, his freeing for the future. And according to the prior death of Jesus Christ the resurrection has this negative presupposition in a radical turning of man from his old existence, in a total removing of man in his earlier form, in his absolute putting off, in his complete freeing from the past. It is in this correspondence that we see their difference but also their relationship—which is, of course, necessarily a differentiated relationship' (p. 342, ET, p. 310).

Barth introduces 'a subtle nuance into the understanding' of the relationship between the crucifixion and the raising of Jesus Christ, when he considers the fact that in accordance with the testimony of the scripture concerning the three days between the death and the resurrection of Jesus, the two events are placed, as 'temporal events' in the relationship of events which are 'with' and 'after one another in time' (p. 344; ET, p. 312). They are 'together in time' since the resurrection of Jesus Christ is the exaltation of his former existence, lived for the sake of death on the cross, into a destiny which has taken place once and for all and which as such fills and dominates every present moment throughout time; 'His history did not become dead history. It was history in His time to become as such eternal history' (p. 346, ET, p. 313). Here Barth adopts in a positive sense the teaching of ancient dogmatic theology concerning the high priestly office of Christ in the state of exaltation (pp. 346f., ET, pp. 313f.). Being together in time in this way, the crucifixion and resurrection, that is, the risen Christ who 'as the Crucified . . . "lives and reigns to all eternity" (Luther)' (p. 345, ET, p. 313), form for men in every age 'the basis of the alteration of their situation' (p. 348; ET, p. 316).

In the fact that they are 'after one another in time' Barth finds the basis of the temporal relationship of the Church in the world to its Lord who is present. Since the Church understands the presence of the risen Christ as making this the age of his Church, it interprets the age in which he exists on the basis of the presence of the risen Christ in time; and by understanding the presence of the risen Christ as laying down the limits of this age as the age of the Church, it interprets its own age in terms of the presence of the risen Christ at the end of time, and as forming the final phase of time. In a terminology which may perhaps sound awkward, one may say that in asserting that the crucifixion and resurrection are 'together in time' Barth brings into relief the identity in substance of the saving presence of the crucified and risen Christ, which is the principle by which the situation of all men at every age is altered to their good by God; by saying that they are 'after one another in time' Barth draws attention to the different modes in which the crucified and risen Christ is present to save, this being the presence which inaugurates and brings into being the age in which the Church of Jesus Christ can exist as the fellowship of men who have begun to live in thankfulness and hope, because of the change in their position brought about by God. The age that has begun is the age of the mediated presence of the risen Christ between the 'first *parousia*' of Jesus Christ which began in the days of the resurrection, 'in virtue of which he . . . is the One . . . who has come, who is present', and 'his final *parousia*, in which . . . he is the One who will be revealed . . . at the end and as the end of all time and history', and in which he is 'the One who is to come' (p. 367; ET, p. 333).

4. Only after Barth has expounded at great length the differentiated link between the crucifixion and resurrection does he introduce, as his fourth point, the reality of the event of the raising of Jesus Christ from the dead, as the first of two 'formal but important' complementary issues (p. 368, ET, p. 333). The second forms (5) the fifth point, in which he sets out the unity of the crucifixion and resurrection as a unity in a sequence moving in an irreversible direction, need not be examined more closely here (pp. 378ff., ET, pp. 312ff.). Under his fourth point, Barth explains of the resurrection of Jesus Christ, with great emphasis, that 'it has happened in the same sense as His crucifixion and His death, in the human sphere and human time, as an actual event within the world with an objective content' (p. 368, ET, p. 333). One cannot fail to see at whom this statement is aimed, and yet this thesis is not given the status of an axiom, but merely that of a 'complementary issue'. For all that is done here is that, as a logical consequence of the significance of the assertions made under the first and second points, they are given the force of criticisms of opposing views on the assumption of the differentiated connexion

developed in the third point;[9] and special attention is drawn to the theme that the raising of Jesus Christ, as God's new act of revelation, separate from the atonement through the death of Jesus Christ on the cross, imparts to us a form of existence distinct from and in contrast to human life. Barth believes that he is one with the testimony of the New Testament in the assertion that what happens is not something within us, within our consciousness or our life, but something outside us, something that happens objectively. But this again is not something which takes place beyond the dimension in which we live as men, receive our experiences and attain knowledge, but within this realm in the reality of the world of space and time. Consequently, he insists on the dual characteristics of something which is both objectively outside us, and also within the world of space and time, though at the same time this does not lead him to lose sight of the distinctive nature of the event of the resurrection, by contrast with the crucifixion. He is well aware 'that as we pass from the story of the passion to the story of Easter we are led into a historical sphere of a different kind' (p. 369, ET, p. 334), the peculiar nature of which is not concealed by the New Testament witnesses, but proclaimed unequivocally, in the very uniqueness of its assertions. 'The death of Jesus Christ can certainly be thought of as history in the modern sense, but not the resurrection' (p. 370, ET, p. 336). But only on the assumption that the category of the historical is a necessary condition which must be satisfied by all that takes place within space and time for it to exist as such, can this assertion imply the conclusion that the event of the resurrection was not an event in space and time. Barth sees no more compelling reason for accepting the validity of this assumption than he does for working out an analogy of events in space and time, into which the distinctive nature of the event of the resurrection could be fitted. On the contrary, both these possibilities are excluded for him by the substance of the event of the resurrection, which consists in the fact that it was an act of God, which can only be revealed and known as such, and which is therefore totally misunderstood, whenever reflection upon it comes to regard its specific character as an event in space and time as its real essence,

---

[9] The relationship of the unity of this consequence, as discussed under the fifth point, to the theme of the third point (the differentiated connexion) is similar (*ibid.*, pp. 378ff., ET, 342ff.).

or even attempts to begin consideration of it with this feature. For even Barth's critics should have understood that the statement that the raising of Jesus Christ took place in space and time, 'as an actual event within the world with an objective content', is no more than a consequence of the assertion that it happened 'solely and exclusively as an act of God', as his act of revelation in its entirety, and that the relationship between the two assertions must never be inverted in such a way as to draw from the occurrence of the raising of Jesus Christ in space and time the consequence that to this extent it was an act of God. This would be to share the same coarse misunderstanding of the resurrection as a confirmatory miracle, on the level which Barth is as determined to abolish as Bultmann, and from which in fact he keeps his statements free by virtue of the irreversible direction in which their arguments proceed.

If one should ask why Barth insists so vehemently upon the concrete objectivity of the events of the resurrection, one stumbles upon an issue which has already been noted as a criticism of Bultmann, that of the distinction between providing of a basis for faith and its coming into being. 'The texts do not speak primarily of the formation of the Easter faith as such but of its foundation by Jesus Christ Himself, who met and talked with His disciples after His death as one who is alive (not outside the world but within it), who by this act of life convinced them incontrovertibly of the fact that He is alive and therefore of the fact that His death was the redemptive happening willed by God. According to the texts this event of the forty days, and the act of God in this event, was the concrete factor in its externality, its objectivity, not taking place in their faith but in conflict with their lack of faith, overcoming and removing their lack of faith and creating their faith' (p. 376, ET, p. 341).

In fact if the two conceptions are carefully examined, the true difference between Barth and Bultmann in their views of the resurrection is not that one is orthodox and affirms the reality of the resurrection of Christ, while the other is unorthodox and denies it, as is widely supposed, but that in an historical perspective, Bultmann speaks of the events of Easter only as the rise of faith in the saving efficacy of the cross of Jesus Christ, while Barth understands and expounds the resurrection of Jesus Christ as providing of the basis of faith, distinct from the act of faith.

The limits placed by this historical starting point upon Bult-mann's statement that faith in the resurrection is 'faith in the saving efficacy of the cross' has been recognized by E. Fuchs, who indeed accepts the statement 'as the summary assertion of an objective expositor' but goes on to add that 'the statement nevertheless requires, and I trust that Bultmann is in full agree-ment with me here, to be extended or corrected'.[10]

He goes on to pose the question in answer to which this neces-sary addition is the answer: 'How far can the cross be understood as the saving event?' (p. 297). Basically this is the very question which Barth's exposition seeks to answer: the cross of Jesus Christ can be understood as a saving event, insofar as God him-self, through the act of the resurrection, constitutes Jesus Christ himself, the risen Christ, as the compelling witness to his own cross as the decisive saving event, thereby making him the first and the ultimate basis of faith. Naturally, the term 'the basis of faith' does not mean an assumption which makes faith partially or wholly superfluous, either in the sense that it allows someone to attain more easily to faith, or in the sense that it is a basis which can be confirmed as the basis of faith outside faith, as, for example, by the methods of historical investigation. G. Ebeling explains this in somewhat formal terms: 'Rather, the ground of faith is that which makes faith what it is and so maintains it that it really remains faith—in other words, that on which faith in the last resort depends.'[11] But we must go on to say that precisely because faith constantly depends upon it, the basis of faith must be independent in nature, in order that without being dependent upon faith, it may call faith into being and give it its substance. With this transcendence of the basis of faith by contrast with faith itself, signifying that it subsists independently of faith, and con-stituting its concrete objectivity, there is necessarily associated the further point that the basis of faith is accessible and evident as a basis only to faith, which can be expressed by saying that the basis of faith is the actual object of faith. Thus the objectivity of the basis of faith has a specific double significance: on the one

[10] E. Fuchs, 'Das Sprachereignis in der Verkündigung Jesu, in der Theologie des Paulus und im Ostergeschehen', 1959, in *Zum Hermeneutischen Problem in der Theologie. Die existentiale Interpretation* (1959), p. 297.

[11] G. Ebeling, 'Die Frage nach dem historischen Jesu und das Problem der Christologie. R. Bultmann zum 75. Geburtstag, 1959', in *Wort und Glaube* (1960), p. 317 (ET, *Word and Faith* [1963], p. 304).

hand, it signifies the real independence of the basis of faith from faith itself, the fact that it subsists in itself and is not dependent upon faith, so that it is better to speak of it as the basis *for* faith; on the other hand it signifies that it is evident and accessible to faith and to faith alone. In other words, in the relationship of the basis of faith to faith, transcendence in the ontological plane and immanence in the epistemological plane are associated in such a way that in fact the two elements are inseparably linked, but nevertheless must be precisely distinguished by theological thought, if we are not to arrive either at a theory of isolated saving facts, or a theory of absolute faith.

II

A second type of interpretation of the New Testament tradition of the resurrection, in a form which has been very carefully thought out methodologically, is represented by W. Marxsen, in his study 'The Resurrection of Jesus as a Historical and Theological Problem'. The study consists of three parts: (1) A historical analysis of the coming into being of the primitive Christian doctrine of the resurrection of Jesus (pp. 15-31 above). (2) A systematic analysis of the meaning of the New Testament statement concerning the resurrection of Jesus (pp. 31-44). (3) A systematic reflection upon the justification for the theological statement of the resurrection of Jesus (pp. 44-50).

A. Marxsen locates the starting point for the historical derivation of the primitive Christian *kerygma* of the resurrection in the literary category of New Testament narratives of *appearances* in which 'only the fact of the appearances as such is mentioned'. In other words: 'At the beginning of the tradition there is the mere claim to have seen Jesus who was crucified' (p. 26). The result of the study of the extant literary record of these visions in the New Testament leads Marxsen to the general statement: 'We can say quite confidently that it did happen that witnesses saw Jesus who was crucified. We must express more precisely. Witnesses claim, after the death of Jesus, to have seen him' (p. 30). The primary datum, beyond which historical analysis cannot continue its inquiry, consists of the Easter experience, or as Marxsen terms it, the 'vision which happened' to the first witnesses.

'On the basis of this vision, which witnesses claim to have

happened to them, they then, by a process of reflective interpretation, arrived at the statement: Jesus has been raised by God, he is risen' (p. 30). If this assertion is merely an 'interpretative statement made use of by those who reflected on what had happened to them (at that time)', (p. 31) then the conclusion of a historical inquiry into the factual nature of Jesus' resurrection must end with the statement that on principle *non liquet*. For 'in historical terms, it can only be established that people after Jesus' death claimed that something had happened to them which they described as seeing Jesus, and reflection on this happening led these people to the *interpretation* that Jesus had been raised from the dead' (p. 31).

B. In his systematic analysis of the significance of this interpretative statement Marxsen accounts the distinction between primary experience and secondary reflection as of decisive relevance. It is relevant insofar as the fact that early witnesses, using the concept of the resurrection of the dead, were applying traditional apocalyptic material to interpret their original experience, need not of itself imply that this category of thought, or the apocalyptic tradition as such, must be exclusively taken into account in an interpretation. Rather, Marxsen believes it possible to isolate a tradition in the New Testament itself, in which the fundamental resurrection experience is expressed in a quite different way. According to Marxsen, the ancient credal formulae I Cor. 15.3-7 and Luke 24.34 show 'that both the setting up of the community as well as the reasons given for functioning within it were traced back to a vision of Jesus after his crucifixion. Now this means what supplies the real basis of the community and the functions within it is *the fact*, not of the resurrection itself, but of Jesus' *appearances* . . .' (p. 34). To support his thesis that in these formulae it is 'wholly' the appearance of Jesus and not the fact of the resurrection of Jesus which are being 'brought into prominence' (p. 34), Marxsen uses the passages I Cor. 9.1; Gal. 1.15f.; Matt. 28.16; John 20.19-23 and Acts 10.40-42, where the 'experience of the appearance' seems still to be primarily and directly associated with the theme of the sending of the disciples. The consequences of the founding of the community and certain injunctions which have to be observed by it or in it, consequences which in the tradition are associated with the appearances of Jesus, are seen by Marxsen as 'likewise interpretative derivations' from the original Easter experience, and as (at least in principle) independent of the other interpretative derivation, that of the resurrection from the dead.

'We can therefore state that the experience of the appearances come to be spoken of in two ways' (p. 36), or in other words, that 'the experience of the vision is found in two explanatory contexts, each of which points in a different direction' (p. 36).

In the first case, the interpretation leads backwards to the assumptions of the Easter experience; this reflective interpretative theory is retrospective in form, and with the help of apocalyptic tradition, is articulated in the assertion of the resurrection of Jesus. In the second case, the process of interpretation looks forward to the consequence of the Easter experience; this anticipatory interpretative theory reaches forward into the future, and can be summarily described as being brought to realization in the mission of the Church. In the first case the 'experience of the vision of Jesus' is followed by a reflection on what had gone before, while in the second case 'the experience brings into being a function' (pp. 36f.). Marxsen sums this up by the statement that 'both the reflection and the function have a common starting point, namely, the claim that the vision had happened. But what had happened "came to be spoken of" in opposite directions' (p. 37).

Marxsen's aim in so distinguishing the two interpretative theories on the basis of the differentiation he lays down between direct experience and the mediated formulation of that experience (mediated either by the reflection and the tradition of the first witnesses, or by the functions and mission of the Church), becomes obvious when the two interpretations are examined with regard to their content. For here Marxsen gives unequivocal prominence as an hermeneutic principle to the anticipatory interpretation, the nature of which he has previously described by the term 'the bringing into being of a function'. A first step towards qualifying these functions takes place with the cautious observation: 'It was probably in the first place a question of preaching' (p. 37).

While Marxsen is still firmly in touch with the text of the New Testament, he is obliged in what follows to advance theses which it seems very difficult to verify exegetically, since he asserts that the content of the preaching which was begun by the appearances of Jesus after his crucifixion is neither the resurrection experience, that is, the 'experience of the appearance of Jesus' itself, nor a truth of which this was the very first manifestation (p. 37). By making use of John 20.21 ('As the Father has sent me, even so I send you') as his guide, Marxsen arrives at the positive thesis that the original Easter experience gave rise to the conviction that the event which had begun with the beginning of Jesus' ministry was being continued; that is, the presence of God, as the fundamental event in history and in time underlying faith, was being continued. Marxsen formulates the relation between the events of the resurrection experience and the 'historical Jesus' in these words: 'Jesus' "purpose", having been set in motion by the vision which was experienced, . . . is carried on by his witnesses. In their functions, they now take the place of Jesus' (p. 37).

'The content of the function' brought into being 'by the vision' is described by Marxsen 'in the first instance and provisionally' by the phrase 'the purpose of Jesus is continued' (p. 38). Put somewhat more precisely, this signifies that the central and real concern of the founding and sending forth of the Church brought about by the appearance of Jesus is 'the continuing occurrence of the *kerygma of Jesus*' (p. 38). According to this, the significance of the resurrection experience is that the essence of Jesus, which consists of the presence of God in Jesus' *kerygma*, and which began with the beginning of the historical ministry of Jesus, is still present and at work, whenever and as long as men acclaim it 'today' and thereby claim time to live. 'We might sum up briefly by saying that the content of the interpretative theory that the resurrection brings into being a function, is that "he still comes today" ' (pp. 38f.).

By contrast, Marxsen characterizes as essentially secondary the retrospective interpretation of the resurrection of Jesus, where we have to do with 'not a statement about functions, but a statement about a *person*' (p. 39); at best it gives us information concerning 'the *belief-of* those who had carried out (with the aid of *their* conceptions) this process of reflection' (p. 39). But the belief summed up in the statement: 'Jesus was raised from the dead by God' can only become relevant to others 'when the reflection once again brings into being a function' (p. 40), that is, when the retrospective judgment concerning the resurrection of Jesus is deciphered and expressed in plain language, which signifies that the 'purpose of Jesus' did not come to an end with his death, 'but . . . still holds good today' (p. 40). Put more precisely, this means that to speak of the resurrection of Jesus has its sole and real significance in the fact that Jesus' *kerygma* is uttered as urgently in the world, even after the cross and beyond the death of Jesus, as Jesus himself originally proclaimed it. Here the primacy, as a hermeneutic principle, of the anticipatory and functional interpretation over the retrospective and personal interpretation, as Marxsen conceives it, becomes clear. The retrospective reflection which terminates in the assertion of the resurrection of Jesus has no independent significance here, but only that of a 'guarantee' or 'substantiation', by comparison with the prolongation of Jesus' *kerygma* beyond his death. Consequently, the original purpose of the retrospective statement concerning the resurrection is that 'it is intended to provide the reason why after Good Friday it is still possible and right to commit ourselves to the "purpose" of Jesus, that is, because he has indeed been raised' (p. 40).

C. By subordinating the statement concerning the resurrection of Jesus to the continuation of Jesus' *kerygma*, Marxsen has already decided the *quaestio iuris* with respect to the theological doctrine of the resurrection. For the question of the legitimacy of this statement is that of the relationship between the ministry of the historical Jesus and the concept of the resurrection of the dead; that is, it takes the form of a choice between whether the ministry of Jesus determines the concept of the resurrection, or whether this concept determines what can be said of Jesus. That Marxsen chooses the first possibility, and not the second, is merely a consequence of his previous exposition. In accordance therewith, 'it is not the idea of the resurrection which forms a *Leit-motiv* into which Jesus should have been or was in fact fitted. The *Leit-motiv* was Jesus himself. He had first been crucified, but then had been seen. Now the concept of the raising of Jesus was merely one interpretative theory—and only one among others— by the help of which what had happened was reflected upon and brought to utterance' (p. 47). To support his choice, Marxsen appeals to 'the (original!) traditions' in the New Testament, which speak of a ministry of Jesus 'which in itself raised an eschatological claim, but which did not demand ratification' (p. 47), that is, it required no further definition. As Marxsen puts it, 'Jesus was experienced in his earthly ministry as an anticipation of the *eschaton*, as a divine event' (p. 47). And he goes on to say: 'This divine event, bound up with him, which was finished once he was dead, was brought into being once again by the fact that he had been seen' (p. 47).

It is therefore only consistent for Marxsen to make the pointed declaration 'that the raising of Jesus is not the fundamental *datum* of Christianity' (p. 47). For even though the continuation of the 'purpose of Jesus' by the Church is set in motion and brought about by the resurrection experiences, the basis and justification for its continuation is found solely in the eschatological actuality, incommensurate with any time within this world, of the essence of Jesus as the presence of God. Thus according to Marxsen 'the question of the resurrection of Jesus is not that of an event which occurred after Good Friday, but that of the earthly Jesus, and the question, inseparably linked with it, of how this purpose later became a reality of experience, which can still be experienced today' (p. 50); that is, the problem of the resurrection is the twofold problem of the earthly Jesus and the Church's preaching in accordance with the eschatological nature of Jesus himself.

III

A third position in the theological discussion of the theme of the resurrection of Jesus Christ has been adopted by W. Pannenberg; he himself regards his central 'thesis, that the resurrection of Jesus is the basis of an understanding of his divinity, i.e. in the first instance of the revelation of God in him' as an 'opposition to the way in which in present day theological study christology is normally built up "from below" '.[12]

Nevertheless, the starting point of this antithesis is the common basis of the programme for the 'christology "from below" ' which theologians from Schleiermacher to Ebeling have sought to construct. For even for Pannenberg, it is an inevitable postulate that 'christology must begin with the man Jesus' (p. 30). It becomes in fact an irrefutable axiom: 'Christology must proceed from Jesus as he was' (p. 42). Given this starting point, however, the 'specific nature of the christological question concerning Jesus' must be strictly preserved, 'that is, that its starting point is

[12] W. Pannenberg, *Grundzüge der Christologie* (1964), p. 106.

not some purely provisional aspect of his acts and words, his effect upon men, but his relationship to God, as it is expressed in the whole of his ministry' (p. 30). In spite of the shared assumption that the starting point of christology must be the historical Jesus, and that its goal must be the relationship of Jesus to God, Pannenberg's opposition to most modern attempts to produce a christology 'derived from the study of the historical Jesus' consists in the question of the substantiation of the specific relationship of Jesus to God. The basic answer given by Pannenberg is that 'the unity of Jesus with God is not already substantiated by the claim implied by his pre-resurrection ministry, but only by his resurrection from the dead' (p. 47). In this fundamental thesis, Pannenberg disassociates himself from all present day christological conceptions, in which 'the unity of Jesus with God is substantiated not by his resurrection, but by the claim to possess authority of his preaching and of his will' (p. 47). Typical of these are not merely the dogmatic essays of W. Elert (1940), P. Althaus (1947) or F. Gogarten (1948), but equally the new exegetical approach to the historical Jesus since about 1950.

Insofar as in these the basis and norm of all christological statements are sought exclusively in the words and acts of the earthly Jesus, Pannenberg by contrast emphasizes the 'proleptic aspect of the claim to authority of the pre-resurrection Jesus' (p. 47) which is 'made visible by the tension between the present and the future in the preaching of Jesus' (p. 53). This proleptic character makes it impossible to hypostatize the 'claim of Jesus to be the presence of God' (p. 52), and defines it as 'an anticipation of a ratification which is only to be expected in the future' (pp. 52f.). Symptomatic of this is the saying concerning the Son of man (Luke 12.8f. and parallels), which he regards as a genuine saying of Jesus, and which contains a strict correlation between the present attitude of men to Jesus and the future decision of the Son of man concerning them. On this basis it becomes evident to Pannenberg that the 'presence of salvation in the whole message and ministry of Jesus' is 'an anticipation of the future judgment. This is the proleptic structure of the claim of Jesus' (p. 55).[13]

[13] For a criticism of the proleptic conception cf. G. Klein, *Theologie des Wortes Gottes und Hypothese der Universalgeschichte. Zur Auseinandersetzung mit Wolfhart Pannenberg*, Beitrag zur Ev. Theol., Vol. 37, [1964], pp. 38ff.

According to Pannenberg, it contains the decisive implication 'that the notable tension between the fact that the end of the world is in the future, while the final decision is present in the person of Jesus, opens the door to the question of the authentication of the claim of Jesus' (p. 52). The specifically anticipatory character of the ministry of Jesus means that this ministry is not merely basically identical in form with the historical pattern of late Jewish apocalyptic, but also with the inner form of Old Testament prophecy. Pannenberg writes: 'Jesus' claim to authority, by its proleptic structure, corresponds to the historical form taken by apocalyptic visions, which in their turn go back to the reference to the future found in the prophetic oracles. The prophets receive words which must be confirmed by their fulfilment in the future and demonstrated as words of Yahweh. The historical visions of the apocalyptic visionaries, which similarly anticipated future events, required confirmation by the course of events itself' (p. 55). For all the differences between the historical Jesus and the apocalyptic visionaries of late Judaism, 'apocalyptic remains the intellectual horizon not merely of the Baptist's preaching of repentance . . . but also of the anticipation of the kingdom of God by Jesus' (p. 56). This basic formal similarity between the structure of Jesus' ministry and the standard pattern of late Jewish apocalyptic is very important for Pannenberg, since it confirms his view of the 'proleptic character' of the claim of Jesus which 'required ratification in the future' (p. 57). According to Pannenberg the 'question of the authentication of his claim to authority' (p. 58) is, as a question, an essential constituent element in Jesus' ministry; for, in his view, the 'whole ministry of Jesus remained dependent upon the future authentication of his claim to authority, upon a confirmation which Jesus himself was no longer able to provide . . . because and to the extent that it was a question of the legitimation of his own person, which was linked with the coming to pass of the final event which he had foretold' (p. 59).

This formal pattern of the necessity of the future legitimation of a present event provides the perspective in which Pannenberg considers the raising of Jesus. Essentially this signifies that 'Jesus' claim to authority cannot be taken in isolation as the basis of a christology, as though all that mattered was a "decision" concerning him. Such a christology, and the preaching based upon it, would be in essence an empty assertion. What everything really depends upon is the question of the connexion between the claim of Jesus and its ratification by God' (p. 61). This question was answered in the resurrection of Jesus Christ. If in what he preached Jesus basically shared the spirit of apocalyptic, then it is possible for Pannenberg to argue that the 'expectation of the earthly Jesus' looked forward to 'the imminent and general resurrection of the dead' (p. 61). And 'when the disciples of Jesus then encountered the risen Christ, there is no doubt that they too understood this as the beginning of the general resurrection of the dead, as the beginning of the events of the end of the age' (p. 61). The 'connexion between the raising of Jesus and the final event of the general resurrection from the dead and the judgment' (p. 61) has an essential formative function in Pannenberg's concept, because in this view the 'significance originally inherent in the event of the raising of Jesus' cannot be other than that 'which belongs to it within its original context in the history of the tradition, that is, in the framework of the apocalyptic future hope' (p. 62).

In this framework, the resurrection of Jesus appears as the onset of the eschatological resurrection of the dead; and at the beginning of the event of the end of the age, brought about by God himself, it legitimizes the claim to authority made by Jesus in his ministry before the resurrection. Pannenberg strongly emphasizes that the event of the resurrection of Jesus itself cannot be thought of and affirmed as an isolated fact with no conceptual context or known meaning. Rather, he emphasizes, 'this fact, insofar as it is understood in its own framework in the history of tradition, has its own proper significance: the onset of the end, the confirmation and exaltation of Jesus by God himself, and the final proof of the deity of the God of Israel, as the one God of all men. Only because a "language" exists for describing this event, is it possible for it to be the basis of faith, without an additional and external interpretation having to be imposed upon it' (p. 69).

The logical consequence of this is the view that there is an inner mutual relationship between the apocalyptic hope of the future resurrection of the dead, and the Christian doctrine of the resurrection of Jesus as something which has already happened. This future hope is the hermeneutic assumption for the acceptance and understanding of the fact of the resurrection of Jesus; while in its turn that fact is the historical ratification of the future hope and the basis of its maintenance in Christian faith (p. 77). Nevertheless, within the mutual relationship the apocalyptic hope has an unmistakable primacy, because the certainty of the fact of the resurrection and the understanding of its significance is unequivocally derived from it and based upon it. Pannenberg himself drew attention to this by remarking that 'the very foundation of Christian faith is at issue . . . when one is discussing the truth of the apocalyptic hope of the future judgment and the resurrection of the dead' (p. 79). And he goes on to state even more clearly: 'The basis on which the understanding of the significance of Jesus rests is always linked to the original apocalyptic framework of Jesus' earthly life . . . if this framework is removed, then the fundamental basis of faith is lost, christology becomes mythology, and it has no further continuity with Jesus himself and with the testimony of the apostles' (p. 79).

'The significance directly inherent in the raising of Jesus' (p. 62), that is, the significance which it derives from his late Jewish apocalyptic environment, is summed up by Pannenberg in six points:

First: 'If Jesus is raised, then the end of the world has begun' (p. 62).

Secondly: 'If Jesus is raised, then for a Jew it can only mean that God himself has confirmed the pre-resurrection ministry of Jesus' (p. 62).

Thirdly: 'By being raised from the dead, Jesus was so closely associated with the Son of man, that the inference was obvious: the Son of man is none other than Jesus who is to come again' (p. 63).

Fourthly: 'If Jesus, being raised from the dead, has been exalted to God, and if the end of the world has thereby begun, then God is finally revealed in Jesus' (p. 64).

The 'transition to the Gentile mission', mentioned as the fifth point, is described by Pannenberg himself as 'a direct consequence of the significance already contained in and implied by the resurrection of Jesus' (p. 68), insofar as he himself observes that the theological justification for the Gentile mission is rooted in the specific meaning of the cross of Jesus Christ, which seems first to have been clearly recognized by Paul. In his sixth and final point, Pannenberg as it were draws attention to the formal side of the reality of the events of the resurrection, when he says: 'What primitive Christian tradition has handed down as sayings of the risen Christ, is to be understood, according to its content, as an exposition of the significance contained in the resurrection itself' (p. 68). Such an exposition is unfolded in the framework of the apocalyptic hope, which in this way once again acts and reveals itself as the sole adequate intellectual basis (*ratio cognoscendi*) for the event of the resurrection of Jesus, on which Christian faith is based.

If the basis of Christian faith lies in the reality of the resurrection of Jesus, then the future hope, as late Jewish apocalyptic conceived of it, is the necessary and only adequate condition for the knowledge of this reality. But the chain of causation extends even further, insofar as the 'conceptual world of apocalyptic' can no longer be understood on its own, and therefore requires a theoretical justification of the truth which it contains, which must at least substantiate 'its basic principle, the expectation of the resurrection of the dead in association with the end of the world and the time of judgment' (p. 78). Pannenberg provides this by having recourse to the situation, which he considers to be a 'universally demonstrable anthropological observation, . . . that the essential destiny of man is not finally fulfilled in the finite nature of his earthly life' (p. 79). For this leads to the consequence 'that it is in the nature of man to hope beyond death' (p. 81), something which can once again be confirmed 'by reflection upon the specific character of human existence, which can be summed up and expressed in the terms of modern anthropology by the concept of the openness of man to the world, of his freedom with regard to his environment' (p. 81).

According to this, a general anthropological situation is required to guarantee the validity of the historical intellectual structure of the late Jewish apocalyptic, which underlies both the original significance and the possibility in principle of the resurrection of Jesus. At this point one may inquire whether there is anything which distinguished these conceptions from a thoroughgoing 'fundamental ontological' proof of the truth of Christian faith, and whether the consequence is avoided of making the resurrection of Jesus, as the declared basis of Christian faith, subject to the historical confirmation of an inherent structural principle in human life, existing independently.

IV

In the course of the inquiry into the original system of reference of the resurrection of Jesus, that is, the question of what provides the framework of reference from which the resurrection of Jesus Christ derives its basic significance and can be understood, we have distinguished three positions which have been adopted in present day theological discussion. In the first case, the essential and constituent context of the meaning of the resurrection is sought by relating the resurrection of Jesus Christ to his crucifixion. In the second case, the decisive context of the assertion of the resurrection of Jesus is provided by referring back to the words and deeds, that is, the *kerygma*, of Jesus in his earthly ministry, the validity of which, beyond his death, for present day man is summed up in this assertion. In the third case the apocalyptic expectation of the divine final age, extended to its utmost limits by the ministry of the earthly Jesus, is accounted to be the fundamental context of the meaning of Jesus' resurrection, its significance and the possibility of its happening, which must be deduced by referring back to the tradition of that expectation.

Looking back on all these views of the subject, it is perhaps permissible to make a summary comparison between them. This naturally will not provide an exhaustive account of the state of the problem, but can only, by means of a certain schematization, prepare the way for a further systematic inquiry in one form or another. One possible starting point which is indicated, among others, is to be found in the fact that among the whole complex of interpretations of the New Testament gospel of the resurrection which we have outlined above, it is possible to distinguish a formal and a material aspect of the problem inherent in the theme of the resurrection of Jesus Christ.

I. The formal problem is due to the fact that the traditional statement, 'Jesus has been raised from the dead', takes the form of a statement concerning reality expressed in the perfect tense. The following are examples of the relationships between the different positions that can be adopted:

A. 1. Bultmann, Marxsen and Pannenberg agree on the basic statement that a statement concerning reality in the perfect tense is only possible as a historical judgment, whereas

Barth argues that this assertion has the rank of a principle in theology.

2. The difference between Bultmann and Marxsen on the one hand, and Pannenberg on the other, lies in the way they apply their common principle to the assertion of the resurrection of Jesus:

(*a*) Bultmann and Marxsen argue that the assertion of the resurrection of Jesus has the form of a reflection upon something else, because it is impossible as an historical judgment.

(*b*) Pannenberg argues that the assertion of the resurrection of Jesus is a statement concerning reality, because it is possible as an historical judgment.

B. 1. Barth and Pannenberg agree in advancing the thesis that the assertion of the resurrection of Jesus is a statement concerning reality.

2. They differ in the way they elaborate this thesis, insofar as:

(*a*) Barth affirms that the assertion of the resurrection of Jesus is indeed a statement concerning reality, but is not a historical judgment; while

(*b*) Pannenberg affirms that the assertion of the resurrection of Jesus is a statement concerning reality, because and insofar as it is possible as a historical judgment.

C. 1. Bultmann and Marxsen agree, differing in this from Barth and Pannenberg, that the assertion of the resurrection of Jesus is a statement which is a reflection upon something else.

2. Bultmann and Marxsen differ, however, in specifying the matter upon which it is a reflection, insofar as:

(*a*) For Bultmann this consists of the cross of Jesus, while

(*b*) For Marxsen it consists of the ministry of Jesus (the reflection being brought about by the fact that the disciples of Jesus saw their master after his death).

Thus the formal problem of the theme of the resurrection of Christ can be summarized and set out as a twofold question:

1. Whether the assertion, which has been handed down in the form of a statement concerning reality, that 'Jesus has been raised from the dead', is valid as a statement concerning reality, and

2. Whether this validity, if it does in fact possess it, can be and must be perceived in the form of a historical judgment.

II. The material problem of the theme of the resurrection of Jesus Christ, which arises from the examination of the original context and real environment in which the theme obtained its meaning, is closely related to the idea of a christology 'from below', that is, with the question of the necessity and possibility of such a christology. A summary of the relationship between the various views on the subject can be made as follows:

A.   If a christology 'from below' means that all statements concerning Jesus Christ (1) in his relationship to God, or more precisely, in the relationship of God to him, and (2) in his relationship to mankind, and further, as a consequence, in the relationship of individual human beings to him (which is always a relationship in him, that is, in the Church as his body), derive from the historical Jesus and must be based upon knowledge of him, then the position adopted by Bultmann and Barth implies the unconditional denial of the possibility and necessity of a christology 'from below'. The differences in their views, and the different exposition and definition of the denial which results therefrom, may be ignored insofar as their common starting point and goal is the word of God, which has still to be preached by the Church to all men, which has already been believed by some men in the Church, and which as a message worthy of being uttered and believed, as speaking of God, has been introduced into this world of ours once for all by the cross and resurrection of Jesus Christ.

B. 1. By contrast, Marxsen and Pannenberg agree:
(*a*) In postulating a christology 'from below';
(*b*) In regarding the cross as an objective apparent (Marxsen) or actual (Pannenberg) inhibition of the truth of Jesus, that is, of the divine legitimation of the attitude adopted in his words and actions by the earthly Jesus.
2. The differences between Marxsen and Pannenberg are as follows:
(*a*) They differ in working out their christology 'from below' with regard to the value or nature they accord to the truth of Jesus.

i) Marxsen advances the thesis that this truth of Jesus was and has remained wholly and entirely self-sufficient, that is, that it is evident in itself, and effective of itself.

ii) Pannenberg advances the thesis of the proleptic character of the truth of Jesus: that is, that the ministry of the earthly Jesus was not already wholly sufficient in itself, but still depended upon a divine legitimation from outside.

(*b*) They differ in their conception of the resurrection as the removal of the inhibition imposed upon the truth of Jesus by his crucifixion:

i) According to Marxsen, the event of Easter, by which the truth of Jesus was made subjectively evident, is not the divine justification of this truth, but the cause and the beginning of its continued assertion.

ii) According to Pannenberg the event of Easter is an historical fact which is the divine justification of the truth of Jesus, and the sole and only adequate basis for the acknowledging and disseminating it.

Representatives of the United Churches in Baden, Hessen-Nassau, Hessen-Waldeck, and the Palatinate and the Reformed Church in Lippe took part in the work of the Theological Commission. The interest of these churches shows that the Theological Commission of the Evangelical Union Church has taken on an important task for the Church. Meanwhile, the urgency of this task has become ever more clear. Questions which were previously discussed only in narrow academic circles have now attracted the attention of a wider audience, and have become the object of public debate.

By publishing these papers at this early stage of the work of the Commission, we hope to encourage groups among the clergy to meet and work through the papers, testing them against the witness of the Holy Scripture. If opinions are forwarded to the Chancellery of the Evangelical Union Church, they can be taken into consideration in the further work of the Commission.

Joachim Beckmann
President of the Council of the
Evangelical Union Church

INDEX OF NAMES

INDEX OF BIBLICAL REFERENCES